GIRL,
GROOMED

GIRL, GROOMED

A THERAPIST'S MEMOIR OF TRAUMA

CAROL ODELL, LICSW

SHE WRITES PRESS

Published 2025
Printed in the United States of America
Print ISBN: 978-1-64742-872-3
E-ISBN: 978-1-64742-873-0
LCCN has been applied for

For information, address:
She Writes Press
1569 Solano Ave #546
Berkeley, CA 94707

Interior Design by Andrea Reider

She Writes Press is a division of SparkPoint Studio, LLC.

IN HONOR OF:

Gary Sall
(1946–2018)

With gratitude for your legacy.

TABLE OF CONTENTS

AUTHOR'S NOTE

I have changed some of the names and combined some details related to the girls at the stables to protect their privacy.

HIS STORY

He told a story with his whole body. As his deep voice painted the picture, his sun-soaked arms would gesture with maestro-like emphasis. His bushy eyebrows would dance little jigs during the well-timed pauses. His blue eyes would spear into our shy glances for added effect. All while we, a collection of ponytails, cut-off jeans, freckles, and bandanas, sat on hay bales or stood next to stall doors listening intently to his words braid boastful strands of his past into the present. He was always a mesmerizing orator.

"Ya know, I taught William Faulkner to ride," he'd begin, then add details about how he introduced the renowned Southern writer to the world of horses. "Saved him once too." And off he'd launch into telling us about the time Faulkner, tired of convalescing in his upstairs bedroom from a broken leg, asked our storyteller to transport him down to the main floor.

"It would've been no problem carrying him if the heel of my boot hadn't caught on that there top step." Knowing that the two of them were in danger of tumbling down the entire flight of stairs, our protagonist leapt out into open space cradling his famous passenger.

"Still had ahold of him in my arms when I landed. Missed them steps altogether and got us to the bottom in one piece. Could've broke both our necks. That's one of the reasons he signed that picture hangin' in the tack room—that and for teachin' him to ride," he'd conclude with a puffing up of his barrel chest.

Even if I had heard a particular tale many times before, even if I outwardly rolled my eyes, inside, I was caught up in the bravado and charm he exuded in the telling.

"I'm going to write a book about you someday," I would sometimes insert at the end of his stories, my form of applause. I often expressed this intent back when he was my childhood mentor. I imagined writing the story of growing up riding horses in Virginia for what I would call a colorful trainer. I would have cast him as the folklife hero of my story. I would have described the grit and tenacity that helped him learn the horse business from scratch, then to go on to buy his own stables and train riders and jumpers to compete on the show circuit against those with much more money and resources. I would have characterized this as a prevailing-against-all-odds underdog story. It would have been a book about my adoration of this man, my deep abiding love for his horses, and my gratitude for the access he bestowed on those of us who rode for him.

"Well, what are ya waitin' for?" he'd counter with that gold-toothed grin I'd come to associate with approval and later with caution.

What was I waiting for? I didn't realize that the wiser part of me was waiting until the full truth of my narrative could be revealed—first to myself. Back then, I wasn't able to see the entire landscape. My vision was only set to portrait. His portrait, never mine. I surrendered myself to his view of the world, adopting an interpretation that helped me manage the situation. This is the power of conditioning and the strength of our coping strategies.

At that gangly-girl time in my life, my version minimized and downright omitted the abuse and violence that was the main staple of my diet at the stables. It redacted the trauma. But more importantly, out of my experiences I etched a story held within me that distorted reality. When I was still "one of his riders," I couldn't possibly have known that it is a common phenomenon to admire and identify with a sexual abuser and that this misguided high regard goes hand in hand with the abuse of power. But that wasn't the extent of my grooming. My well-intended family, the culture, and my own defenses all played a part in what I absorbed from my childhood and the narratives I internalized as a result. This was self-protective—until it wasn't.

You see, it isn't what happens to us that is the biggest problem. The difficulty has everything to do with how we interpret and absorb what happens to us, whatever that may be. These are the elements that go into creating the narratives that we end up digesting—and regurgitating. Through understanding how this comes about, it allows us to compassionately rewrite and "re-right" our stories. This work frees us.

I am well aware that I am not alone on this journey. As a psychotherapist, I've walked with many brave souls along this path toward liberation and a deeper connection with themselves and the world. I have witnessed over and over again the courage that it takes to disentangle from our adopted stories.

Now the time has come to tell my own story of continuing to understand the effects of trauma and to unravel the conditioned narratives behind it.

CHAPTER 1

SEPARATED

The glass representing my marriage always seemed half full to me—that is, until the moment when my husband told me to move out. We were in the middle of a group therapy session led by our unorthodox therapist, Gary, who was part guru and part samurai in his approach. Being in his unique practice involved participating in groups with other clients while sitting in an unadorned basement room on pillows that sagged under the weight of many heavy sessions. Starting out as strangers, we were all now committed to doing our growth work in these shared circles.

On this particular evening, my husband, Mark, and I were polarized in our conflict about some upcoming decision. In the midst of our swirling dialogue, I blurted out a comment that didn't even register on my radar screen, but the collective silence that followed was palpable by everyone else. The contempt seeping between my words was conveniently bland to me but had just left a bitter residue with Mark, and the witnessing members of our therapy group.

After an elongated pause, he locked his eyes on mine, and with a measured tone, he slowly annunciated, "I want you to go back to the house now and pack your things. I want you out by the time I get home."

I was stunned! I hadn't seen this coming. Mark typically went out of his way to avoid conflict. Our spats wouldn't necessarily feel resolved, but we moved past them quickly. Yet here he was in this moment, holding an intense "I mean it" gaze.

Everything in me wanted to rant in response, *"Really? You are kicking me out of my own house? Because of what?"* From my point of view, this sudden guillotine edict seemed so random, the reason so insignificant. Through our twenty-seven years of marriage we had co-created a satisfying life on the outskirts of Seattle that involved juggling careers, parenting our son, managing a home, and enjoying various activities and friendships. We had well-honed routines and ways of dancing around conflict that worked well enough for both of us. We were living the good life, right? At least I thought so.

Yes, okay, we were here for a second round of therapy with Gary. The first stint had taken place twenty years previously. Mark and I were coming back now, not because we were fighting, but because there were communication problems, which in my opinion could be solved if Mark would only listen more closely. In our return to counseling I had secretly been counting on Gary and the group to address this and Mark's other issues. Being a therapist myself, I, of course, thought I could best diagnose. Instead, I was the one being confronted. I felt unjustly sideswiped by this turn of events.

Attempting to regain my bearings, I found myself pleading. "You want to give all this up? Throw it all away? End our marriage?"

Without taking the bait, Mark held firm. "I'm not asking for a divorce at the moment, but unless things change, that option is on the table."

It was then that any semblance of anger I was harboring morphed into panic-filled shock. *Oh shit! He is serious. This is bad. Where am I going to go?* The tidal wave of realization that my marriage and life were in crisis crashed through my insides as I struggled to grasp my suddenly altered reality.

It was in this disoriented fugue state that I staggered to my feet from the pillowed floor, drove home, gathered a suitcase of miscellaneous clothes, and checked into a hotel until I could sort out what to do next.

CHAPTER 2

NOW WHAT

Here's the thing about a crisis. It's not necessarily a bad thing. Professionally I knew that this is often the wake-up call we need—the moment when we are forced to face the hidden parts of ourselves that have been unconsciously trying to run the show and wreaking intermittent havoc and unhappiness along the way.

And here's the thing about marriage. If you're doing it right, your partner is often the one who has to grab you by the shoulders and plead, "Wake up!" But the other thing about being thrown into a crisis . . . you are never ready for it.

Over the next few days, I zombie-lurched my way into signing a month-to-month lease on a tiny studio apartment that would easily fit into our living room at home. I prayed this arrangement would only be temporary. It was spring of 2015, and as I unpacked my meager things and pulled down the unstable Murphy bed for my first of many sleepless nights, I chafed the worry beads of my mind. *How the hell did this happen to me? What am I going to do now? What if we get divorced? How am I going to tell my friends and family?* Everything in my life had just been pulverized.

In an attempt to regain my footing I reminded myself that I was a good person and I hadn't done anything wrong. Then shame took over. *I'm a marriage counselor for god's sake. And here I am being kicked out of my own home with my own relationship now on the proverbial rocks!* I was deluged by surges of grief, humiliation, and anger—along with a mixture of sensations I couldn't even yet identify. I see-sawed between blaming the injustice of it all as if I were the victim: *I can't believe that Mark would do this to me!* and collapsing into flagellating self-judgment: *I am so fucked up!*

Meanwhile, I was determined to fix things between us. I wanted back in the house, back in my marriage, back in the comfort of the familiar. I could make this right, right? Since Mark had asked for no contact for an undetermined amount of time, the therapy would now consist of individual sessions and separate groups. I started my next appointment with Gary by laying out my plan of action to move up that time frame.

"I'm going to tell Mark that I am sorry, apologize, and commit to prioritizing him," I frenetically began.

Gary quickly cut in. "Not so fast. This is not a problem to be fixed."

"What do you mean?" I asked with an edge of annoyance at being interrupted. "I am trying to save my marriage."

"It doesn't work like that," Gary said.

"I don't understand. How am I supposed to resolve anything if not through throwing myself into doing better?"

I had always been able to set my sights on a goal and work hard to achieve it. This approach had served me well. Couldn't

Gary appreciate that I wanted to be back together with Mark and was ready to go into overtime mode to make this happen?

"You need to slow it down first in order to see what you are up to," he countered.

"I see that I am motivated and committed," I quipped, holding back my irritation that he was somehow missing my intention.

"It's not about getting the outcome you want. It's about deeply observing yourself and what you are up to. This urgency you feel right now is all coming out of your own discomfort, not from a true desire to understand your impact on others." He paused before adding the kicker. "It's completely self-serving."

"That's not fair."

"Stop it," he said. "You are fighting me right now. This is similar to how you act in your marriage too. You are only interested in your point of view and getting what you want."

"Wait, what?" I took in a labored breath.

"You are only driving to get the outcome you want. You don't see that you are being a bully when you do this." His pause then sliced the air between us. "This is the same energy that you bring to your marriage," he continued. "The same energy that ends up running over Mark if he doesn't acquiesce and get on board with your agenda."

I quivered with defensiveness about what was being reflected back to me. I didn't want to see any of this. I didn't want to look at how poorly I had been treating Mark.

"Well, then, what am I supposed to do . . . nothing?" I asked. "Where will that get us?"

Gary went on to try to explain that my problem—and most issues—can't be solved through "over-efforting." This didn't make sense to me at the time. Suddenly disoriented, a whimper escaped. "But this is all I have ever known. This is who I am."

With my well-worn paradigm upended, I felt like I was floundering in turbulent waters, stripped of a life vest. Yikes! The impression of myself that I had always held dear was now gasping for air.

"Ah, now we are seeing another form of your resistance— self-pity," he pointedly observed. "You have had your boot on him, not the other way around. You don't know what to do if you aren't trying to exert control."

Although my catalyzing comment to Mark felt minor to me, I had to admit to myself that it was not altogether unfamiliar. He had previously voiced that he didn't feel like he was appreciated, that I could be quick to put him down, and that I was regularly dismissive of his feelings and requests if they didn't match up with my own. Being challenged now to look at my behavior, I could see that Mark had tried through the years to call me out on the ways I wasn't respecting him as a mutual partner. I could admit that I generally dictated the terms of our marriage. It was apparent in this Hail Mary act that he had been desperately feeling disregarded for years, and it had been convenient for me to overlook this.

It was also true that I could master these arguments. I was a more adept verbal fighter, so any attempt to work through conflict could end up with me debating a better case. Our relationship wasn't a democracy, and my husband had finally reached his limit of bloodletting. The thing I was realizing about continual paper cuts is that you can still bleed out but it just takes longer.

Mark was finally standing up to me in a way that he had been avoiding for years. By asking for this therapeutic separation, the pyramid scheme I had been benefitting from in our marriage had just toppled. He was giving me an opportunity to look at myself in the mirror, but the reflection was so ugly. That difficult session showed me how I had been propping up my ego at his expense. My life shattering around me was breaking me open along with it.

Afterward, I slunk back to my tiny apartment and put up the Murphy bed so that I had space to sit at the miniature table—alone with my feelings. I was too ashamed to reach out to others yet about my depressing circumstances.

Finally with a poppy seed of curiosity, I began to formulate new questions. *If I accept that I am treating Mark like an object of my agenda, how did this happen? How did I come to be like this? How did I become so disconnected? How do I stop inflicting this hurt on the person I say I love? And what does it mean to really love someone?*

Although on the one hand my life circumstances had drastically shrunk, what I was about to unearth would become expansive.

CHAPTER 3

THE HEART OF
HORSE COUNTRY

At the point when my marriage was in serious trouble, I had slipped into believing that I was done with my past. Through a previous chunk of therapy two decades earlier, I thought that I had fully reconciled my old ghosts. I was wrong. I had neglected to remember that a deep understanding of oneself is always a process, never a final destination. Being out of the house was now exposing another sub-layer of unexplored terrain from my childhood. Here was evidence of the detritus of my past showing up unchecked in the present.

When any of the influences in one's life remain unexamined, these same forces tend to come out sideways. I was currently living the upheaval brought about by my unintended yet aggressive actions. Clearly, I needed to take a closer look into my personal history.

Sitting in my small, one-room space, I reflected on how the hell I got here. The formative experiences of my life are all rooted in my love of horses. In fact, I can't remember a time in my girlhood when I wasn't smitten with horses. Even before I had any real exposure to these magnificent creatures, I heard their whispering in my core. And I felt a visceral longing to respond.

What was it about horses? Was it an unconscious urge to relate to my own powerful animal self? Was it the unique spectrum of qualities these creatures embody? Horses are paradoxical. They are wild yet cooperative, independent of spirit yet innately herd-oriented, strong and vulnerable. The passion I felt for them so early on seemed inextricably linked to my own desire for self-discovery, wholeness, and connection.

Those of you who have felt similar hoofbeats in your blood know what I am talking about, for this is the same insatiable need that fills bookshelves and movies with countless stories about horses and the girls who love them.

Whatever the origin, horses were primally imprinted on me from the beginning. Real horses, however, were a rarity in both Wisconsin and Indiana, the states where I split my early school years. So despite begging my father for a horse, my vicarious young girl self instead played with a plastic toy pony and the girl doll in braids that sat atop. While the rider detached from the pony's back along with the various individual parts, there was a satisfying harmony I felt was restored only when the saddle, bridle, hat, and girl were fitted neatly back together again. I also spent time galloping in the yard, imagining myself as a horse whinnying in stride. All this adoration for horses was relegated to my fantasy world until the summer of 1970.

A year after Neil Armstrong and his crew landed on the moon, my father received a professorial teaching job at the University of Virginia. While the world at large had been recently bolstered by the prospect of exciting new frontiers, my family was likewise about to make a historic launch from the Midwest to our own inaugural landing in the rural South in Charlottesville, Virginia. I was ten years old, and with the siren's call of horses already having a hold of me from sinew to spirit, moving to the "heart of horse country" was a dream come true.

As my parents, my younger brother, and I drove toward our destination, the verdant green tapestry of hills and fields that undulated all around us was capped to the west by the Blue Ridge Mountains. And in every direction there were horses! These sleek, tail-swishing graceful creatures grazed and frolicked near split rail wooden fences, bucolic barns, and groves of trees. Watching out the back seat window, I was abuzz with the possibilities.

In a quiet subdivision well outside of town, my parents bought a house. Squatting on the edge of our property just down the gently sloping hill from our new home was a shabby-looking barn and horse stables. To me, it was a utopia. My lifelong yearning to learn to ride, care for, and just be near real horses was now merely a field away.

CHAPTER 4

MEETING THE MARLBORO MAN

A s soon as I could beg them into action, my parents agreed to go with me to meet our neighbor, the owner of the horse stables down the hill. They opted to drive our wood-paneled station wagon via the road. Instead, I chose to take the shortcut and travel on foot through the connecting fields. I was used to randomly roaming the creek and woods behind the house of my old neighborhood, but this was different. Now I was beelining toward a goal.

I skipped through the grassy pasture, but was slowed by the first barbed wire fence when my T-shirt caught on one of the three thorny metal lines. Wooden fences would have been easier to negotiate, but this was not a high-end stable. The barbed wire that outlined some of the fields had a mercurial mind of its own, seemingly flexible on the one hand but also poised to scrape and snag on the other. Is barbed wire to keep in or keep out? I never pondered this back then. Never hesitated to think about what might lie on the other side of this barrier.

When I first laid eyes on him, he was barking out commands to the girls on horses who were orbiting around him from the middle of a riding ring. Well over six feet tall with a bellowing voice, he was also naked from the waist up. Reminding me of a cross between Robert Redford and John Wayne, he reigned large—part ringleader, part primal man-beast. It was hard not to gape at his deep, butterscotch-colored broad chest and muscular belly that were completely exposed to the elements. Rounding out his sparse attire, he wore rugged jeans and well-worn cowboy boots covered in dust from a hard day's work. From the very beginning I was in awe of his stature.

Then he gazed in my direction. When his sky-blue eyes caught mine, I had to quickly look away. When I furtively glanced back, he broke out in a toothy Cheshire cat smile that revealed one upper front tooth made of solid gold. The glinting metal shone brightly in that afternoon sunshine, like a beacon drawing in my moth self.

As a young girl, I had already been groomed by the TV shows I gulped down after school that depicted cowboys. I was spellbound by Sheriff Matt Dillon in *Gunsmoke*, James West on his glamorous *Wild, Wild West* train car, and Little Joe on his ranch in *Bonanza*. Then, of course, there was John Wayne showing off his slow, unflinching swagger at gunpoint. Even the Marlboro Man, who ruggedly rode his way through the frequent tobacco commercials, became an early crush for me. Yes, all my admired action figures wore cowboy boots, holstered guns at their sides, and had obediently tacked horses as their besties.

The rogue individualistic cowboy was the peddled heroic icon. And like a baby bird, I gobbled up what was being offered. This was the constant diet of my girlhood. Our cultural conditioning begins early. It is invisible and insidious.

Falling into line, I couldn't see then that I was being molded to admire white strong men with power. Men who were charming, invincible, fearless—and often took the law into their own hands. It was primetime viewing for me and was the fodder for my unconscious programming. Though I couldn't have known it at the time, these cultural messages were shaping my mind and biases without my awareness or consent.

Moseying up toward the side of the ring that day, I believed that I was seeing the real deal, the Marlboro Man from Albemarle County, my fantasied hero, suddenly come to life. I moved shyly to the railing, cautious and yet intrigued by this imposing man standing within.

When my parents arrived, he strolled over to introduce himself. After a brief exchange of hellos, he turned that glint in his eyes and the sparkling metal in his smile in my direction once again.

"Well, do ya wanna ride or don't ya?" he asked with a mirth echoed in his dancing caterpillar eyebrows.

"What?" I asked. His strong Southern dialect overlapped his words such that they merged into one galloping sentence that, especially in those early days, left me in need of a translator. Turns out it was more than just his words that I had difficulty understanding.

When he said it again, I could only nod. I had never ridden before, not even sat astride a horse. Here I was on the brink of actualizing this dream, and yet the prospect suddenly seemed daunting. Sometimes it can be so scary to finally be offered what we say we have always wanted.

"Katie, run grab Smokey," he bellowed.

And so came my introduction to this dappled, gray-white pony who arrived donning crusted manure stains along one side of his plump body. It was love at first sight.

I watched as this self-assured older—but not that much older—girl tacked this small pony with deft movements. I paid close attention as she guided the steel bit up toward his mouth. Marveled as he opened his jaw on cue to receive the metal as it slid easily into place between his yellowed teeth. Admired how she then pulled the various leather straps up over and around his ears so that his headband lay flat across his forehead, not unlike my own headband that held back my long brown hair. Then she proceeded to buckle the strap under his throat, placed the reins across the length of his neck, and instructed me to hold the strands of leather under his chin while she went to collect the saddle.

I took this opportunity to gently stroke the length of his gray-and-white-flecked face and look into his big dark eyes outlined with white lashes. While patting his neck, I introduced myself and told him that I thought he was the prettiest pony I'd ever seen. I confessed to him that I was new to this, that I had never ridden before. Although lazily chomping at the bit through my quiet monologue, his large, ebony eyes and forward-set ears gave me the sense he was listening intently.

Katie returned with the saddle, hoisted it into place upon his back, and fastened the girth around his belly. Smokey nonchalantly accepted all these actions as routine, which clearly, they were. *If she can do all this with such ease, then I can too*, I thought to myself.

She reclaimed the reins from me and walked my pony into the ring, motioning me to follow. Then she handed us off to him. At this close proximity, I was even more aware of the stark contrast of his tall, barrel-framed man body compared to my lanky, awkward, ten-year-old girl body.

"Come here," he said, directing me to move closer. I was now near enough to smell the mixture of sweat, straw, horse, and man that exuded from him. He indicated that I should grab ahold of the top of the saddle with both hands and bend my left leg. I was more than willing to be directed in all these ways. Interesting, in hindsight, that I gave him carte blanche authority over me from the very beginning.

"On-the-count-o-three."

But on the count of two he caught me off guard and launched me high up into the air, much higher than was necessary, and plopped me down onto the awaiting saddle. My body was suddenly electrified from the surprise factor, but at the same time aware that he had duped me. I wasn't ready, it didn't go as he said it would, and yet, here I was astride a pony because of him.

My heart continued to canter with adrenaline as he showed me how to hold the reins. "Now, turn your hands this way, thumbs-up." Then he took hold of the bridle and walked me once around the ring, Smokey's droopy head bobbing as we all stepped together. This brawny man looked back at me periodically to correct my posture.

"Sit up straight. Point your toes where you're goin'. Heels down. Hold tight here, like this." He showed me what he meant by manually turning my feet forward and pushing my knee into the saddle with his hand to further connect me to my pony. It felt odd to have this strange man manipulating my body with his firm touch, but I was so thrilled to be learning how to ride that nothing else registered.

After one lap he let go and left me to steer Smokey around the ring on my own. It was remedial, but even at this nascent stage I found it empowering. Here I was, getting to ride a real horse! Well, a small pony—but it was so exciting. I reached down to pat his neck with a swell of gratitude.

"C'mon back tomorrow and I'll teach ya to trot," he promised. This was a day of firsts: my first ride, my first lesson, my first encounter with this man who was to become my teacher for the next fifteen years. What I didn't know then was that this same man would also hijack my life and my story for many more decades beyond that.

What also strikes me as curious looking back was my parents' seeming lack of caution. I don't even remember if they stayed for this debut ride. They might have and I was just oblivious to their presence. After all, I was already immersed in my new girl–horse world. However, they certainly offered no objection or resistance. Did they not have any questions about leaving me in this situation with this shirtless man and his derelict stables that were so clearly his empire? Apparently not.

I can see in retrospect what a pivotal moment this was. Yet it went by without my notice and without their concern as they casually took the first step in passing their parenting reins over to him. In re-examining my past as it was now showing up in my marriage, I would need to expand my lens to also include what was behind my parents' complicit hand-off.

Nevertheless, on that summer day at the age of ten, I had just crossed the threshold, barbed wire and all, into another realm—alone.

CHAPTER 5

WHAT IS IT ABOUT GIRLS AND HORSES?

The next day, I was so enthusiastic about returning to the barn that I wolfed down breakfast on the run. My nerve endings tingled with anticipation. Even in my dimly conscious child-self, I knew that horses represented the potential I hoped to develop in myself. Horses seemed to know who they were and where they stood. I longed to feel this same sense of being grounded and belonging in the world.

My excitement about learning to ride also took my mind off my other worries. In another month I would be starting my fifth-grade year at a new school. This thought made my stomach leapfrog. Spending time at the barn was a welcome distraction and definitely how I wanted to devote my remaining summer days.

As I walked through the fields and shimmied more easily through the lines of barbed wire, I hoped I would be allowed to ride Smokey again. My attachment to this pony already seemed like fate, and today he said he'd teach me to trot.

He . . . what was his name again? Clementine? Clarence? Clarentin? No, that wasn't it. Claren-tyne? Why couldn't I remember his name? Why was that so difficult? I'd just have to listen more closely for the pronunciation when I got to the barn.

Little did I realize back then that his name, pronounced "Clarenteen," was imbued with its own cloaking device. I would witness throughout the years to come that everyone, without exception, experienced trouble remembering it. It's an unusual name, yes, but often when names are unique, they become more memorable and not so universally irretrievable. It is strange how even his name created a kind of fog, like it had been infused with the power to confuse. This spell that he, and his name, cast would take many years to break. But back then I still assumed that there was something lacking in me as to why I was unable to recall it. Kids are prone to interpret their world far too personally, but of course I didn't know this at the time.

Now on the edge of the property line, I suddenly saw a formidable-looking Doberman charging toward me and barking ferociously. I had never been around this breed of dog, but I knew it had a scary reputation. As his mahogany-brown body, lean but muscular, bounded in my direction, my body stiffened. As the gap between us closed, my response wasn't fight or flight—it was pure freeze.

As I stood statue-like, the dog finally slowed to a jog and pulled up in front of me. Then he pushed his thin snout into my crotch with a clear ask for a head rub. With the tension releasing from my body, I gently stroked his unnaturally erect ears, and I knew that we would become fast friends.

Catching my breath, I could then take in my surroundings. Ivy Creek Stables, I later learned, was named after the small "crick" that ran into its tiny namesake town further up the road. The stables were a collection of three main buildings and an outdoor ring. The dilapidated upper barn included an echoey grain silo and multiple stalls surrounding a large, covered space, which would have been big enough to host a lively square dance if the neglected structure hadn't been in such a poor state of disrepair. The other two buildings included a lower barn and a tack room full of saddles and bridles.

The training ring was off to one side from these structures, and that day there were a number of riders on horses and ponies already maneuvering clockwise around the perimeter. A few more girls leaned against or sat upon the top rails watching the entertaining action happening within. Some looked to be my age or a few years older, while others were teenagers who appeared to embody a confidence light-years ahead of mine. There were a couple of adult women too. I didn't understand everyone's connection to this place or to each other, but I was curious to find out.

I shyly edged up to the railing to watch the riders inside and admired how they all seemed to move in sync with their mounts with such a fluid grace. I found myself bouncing up and down on my toes. I couldn't imagine then that the excitement I felt being around horses would ever be weaponized against me.

In the midst of it all there he was again, blue eyes a-blazing, gold tooth a-dazzling, cowboy boots a-strutting. And did he ever wear a shirt? His robust body would never go unnoticed, but displaying his bronzed bare chest made it that much more pronounced. I had only seen my father without a shirt when he, on infrequent occasions, timidly entered the cold lake waters during summer vacations in his conservative bathing suit. In contrast, here was this brute of a man, parading proudly around half-naked without a care or second thought. In all the years to come I would only rarely see him fully dressed—even in the dead of winter.

I gripped my hands around the top rail of the ring and watched with rapt interest as Clarentine directed his various riders through a series of jumps, beginning with the ponies.

"Start with the brush, then this here set of poles, then the outside barrels, end with the combination," he commanded. I couldn't follow the jump course instructions but watched as these riders knew just what he was asking.

After the riders on ponies took their rounds, those on horses were up next. He raised the fences in height and put the next set of riders through their paces. I was surprised when he then again raised the jumps and gave these last few riders their directions. This final group was obviously his elite riders who were training to compete over the biggest fences. And to my eyes these obstacles seemed colossal in size.

I had never seen horses jump like that. I watched as he continued to raise the height of the fences with each successive round. While the last rider was rounding the back side of the ring, he surreptitiously ran over and quickly heightened the final jump by propping the heavy bar on the very tippy top of the standard posts into the highest possible configuration. It was now a tower of straight up and down poles that dwarfed me in height. As I stood with anxious anticipation at the side of the ring I realized that the rider wouldn't have seen this coming.

As she rounded the far corner, I saw the surprise widen her eyes and then her shift into a determined focus I'd never witnessed before. She and her horse bore down toward this last fence, and with a strength and agility I didn't know was possible, they hurtled together over the top, landing safely on the other side. Their acrobatic flying was nothing less than captivating.

Although it terrified me to watch this, it was also exhilarating. I knew then that there was no going back. In that moment I secretly vowed that one day this would be me.

His booming voice startled me out of my daydreams. "Well, go on and git tacked up," he said while pointing me to follow after a different girl who was assigned to assist me.

I turned and hurried to catch up. I quietly waited at the gate while she grabbed a string of baling twine and walked out into the field toward the gray pony I could now identify as Smokey. I was delighted that he was going to let me ride him again today. I watched as she threw this meager string around his neck and, just with that bit of connection, led him back through the narrow gate.

The enthralling moment in the ring now past, I became aware of the stickiness of the Virginian humidity that was shoehorning its way into everything: my clothes, skin, lungs, and Smokey's fur. The unfamiliar thickness in the air sandwiched the fresh smell of hay with the fecund odor of manure and infused it with horse sweat. Over time this became a welcome scent to my nostrils, the aroma of earth and equine baked by sunshine. But before I grew accustomed, the effort to breathe felt strangling, the dampness invasive.

Without a word to me, this other girl finished tacking Smokey and handed me the reins. I got the strong impression that she wasn't happy about my being here. I wouldn't come to understand why this was until much later.

Managing to get into the saddle on my own, I took up the reins as I had been shown the day before. I gave my pony a nudge with my heels and tried to get him to walk into the ring. He wasn't having it. When Clarentine saw me having difficulty, he came over, took hold of the bridle, and led us inside the arena. Once he let loose his hold, I was in the driver's seat. Or was I?

After meandering our way around the ring for a while, trying to stay on the perimeter, he told me to give Smokey a kick and urge him into a trot. I squeezed my legs against his sides, then used my heels to lightly nudge his belly, but to no avail.

I remember thinking that I didn't want to hurt Smokey. I tried again to get my docile pony to break into a faster gait, but he seemed plenty content to just keep going at a slow walk.

"Kick him!" came the resounding voice that startled us both. Smokey, in panicked response to his tone, leapt forward into a trot, almost unseating me in the process.

Involuntarily bouncing up and down on Smokey's back, I flopped forcibly against the saddle seat. Meanwhile, although still clutching the reins, my hands and arms flapped up and down, my legs hinging back behind me. It is no wonder that Smokey, getting the signal that I was pulling back on the reins, dialed our movement back to a walk. So much for my first attempt at trotting. Loving horses was innate for me, but learning to ride them would obviously take a bit more practice.

Clarentine laughed, though there was genuine encouragement in his jesting. He directed me to lower my hands by entwining them into the tuft of Smokey's mane so I wouldn't pull back on his mouth. We broke into a trot again. I was surprised by how difficult it was to steady my trampolining body. I was a piston working in exact opposition to Smokey's short-stridden movements. Smokey had clearly been here before and, being the patient teacher that he was, didn't seem to mind the learning curve of the new student currently on his back.

Through Clarentine's instruction I began to anchor the weight in my heels, my hands in his mane, squeeze my knees tightly against the saddle, and connect my legs more firmly to his round body. With practice that day I began to feel into the tempo of Smokey's trot.

Riding was all about finding a fluid rhythm with one's horse, like choreographed music in motion. While at first I was making the equivalent of the scratchy violin sounds eked out by a new pupil, with practice my movements became more melodic with my mounts.

Clarentine didn't waste much time, and by the next day he was instructing me to canter. I immediately discovered that this gait was a different dance altogether and, with it, a whole new sensation for my body to navigate. Unlike the trot, this stride required a deepening of my center of gravity, a pulling down into the saddle, and an aligning with the one, two, three rhythm as opposed to the one-two staccato beat of the trot.

With time, matching my girl body to my horse's body became smoother, and I came to appreciate the distinct sensation of each horse's personality through their unique way of moving in the world. While Smokey's canter felt like being thrown into an energetic cement mixer, Kid, with saddlehorse breeding in his blood, had a canter that felt like swaying in a porch swing on a late summer evening. Fargo, always full of vim and vigor, felt more like bouncing on a pogo stick. Highlander, with his enormous body, pounded the ground with heavy, warrior strides. I would come to cherish the kinesthetic relationship I shared with them all. But back in these initial days I was just trying not to fall off.

Horses now occupied the centerpiece of my life, not just my imagination. I think back about how often I would traipse to the barn feeling unsure of myself, only to be unconditionally greeted by my favorite horses and ponies. The way they extended a reassuring whinny and tactile nuzzle, the way they seemed to see deeply into me with their polished river-rock eyes. It was a healing salve. No wonder as a girl they were my best friends and confidantes. The connection they offered always felt easier than other social minefields of childhood.

It has since been scientifically proven that horses can specifically read and identify the facial expressions of people in the moment. Even further, it has been shown that they can remember these emotions over time. In other words, horses are capable of storing information about the feelings of others and maintaining an awareness that their human friend was angry or sad or joyful in the recent past. This ability was likely developed because horses, as distinct from dogs, for example, are innately prey animals. Through the centuries they have needed to be able to accurately read their surroundings for survival. They adapted these skills in order to live harmoniously within a herd for protection. With this sophisticated aptitude, horses are inherently able to attune to the emotions in others and therefore they are adroit at creating strong bonds.

29

On the human side, the healing role of emotionally supportive service animals has been more fully researched and acknowledged nowadays. The science validates that for people, the relationships with animals decrease blood pressure while increasing oxytocin, the "feel good" chemical. The companionship is literally healing.

I didn't have this confirming data back when I was growing up around horses, but my own emotional experience of the friendship and loyalty that these amazing creatures offered me was all I needed to know. Horses resonated in my marrow, heart, and soul. And the reciprocal relationship felt nothing less than miraculous.

Later, in adulthood, a friend and I would ponder the very first contact between horse and human way, way back in time when all horses feared saber-toothed tigers, humans, and other carnivores. What would have been the circumstances where a horse first paused long enough to consider that this two-legged creature might be capable of something more than predator behavior and that simultaneously this human hunter might think this animal was better befriended than eaten. Musing together, we thought that it was likely a woman who created this first bridge of possibility to the enormous partnership history between horse and human that followed.

This points to the other thing that horses and girls have in common . . . both are prey to predators. But I get ahead of myself.

CHAPTER 6

A BARN BUDDY

Starting school that fall was easier when I discovered that one of the girls at the barn, Kit, was in my grade. We spent as much time as we could get away with talking about horses in our classroom. Who did we predict was going to ride who at the upcoming show? Who was featured in the latest edition of *The Chronicle of the Horse*, the monthly tabloid covering all the equestrian news? What were some good show horse names? Vim and Vigor? Pied Piper? With colored pens we carefully designed and illustrated elaborate jump courses on paper out of sight of our teacher, Miss Maupin. "All things horses, all the time" could have been our motto.

The best part of the day was when we got to meet up after school at the barn and ride our ponies together. We were in love with the personalities and appearances of our brave miniature-sized steeds. The color of their coats, the curves of their strong bodies, the pattern of their blazes, the number of stockinged legs, their soulful eyes . . .

Kit had been riding and winning ribbons in lead line classes since she could sit upright, so she knew the ropes. Given her equestrian expertise, she was more than happy to show me how to dress, how to clean tack, how to braid manes and tails, how to muck out stalls. Keen to learn all that I could, I became her willing apprentice. At ten, we were an inseparable pair.

Meanwhile, Smokey and I grew closer in our friendship too. He trotted up to me when I stood by the fence. He burrowed his velvety nose into my side. He stood quietly while I fussed with washing, brushing, and tacking him. Our love affair was mutual.

When we weren't riding, Kit and I would go to the quiet area of the upper barn and set up jump courses by laying rakes and pitchforks across cinder blocks and upturned buckets. Whatever we could find was incorporated into our course design. Then we would take turns becoming mythical centaurs who jumped fences with girl bodies melded to horse legs. All things equine dominated my waking to sleeping thoughts and visions. And now I had a barn friend who shared my obsession.

Because Kit had grown up at the barn, she seemed less intimidated by Clarentine, but she also knew to give him a wide berth—when that was possible. I was less adept at that early on but quickly learned that it was an important skill to have. I remember clearly one of the first times that I accidentally stumbled onto his radar. Kit and I were walking our ponies around the ring together. She had invited me for a weekend sleepover at her house and my mom had said I could go.

"By the way, I can come on Friday," I innocently blurted out to Kit in my enthusiasm. I didn't think anyone was listening to us, although I should have known by then that nothing got by him, who was, as usual, overseeing his riders from the middle of the ring.

"I bet ya can . . . *come*," he responded, emphasizing the last word. My confused reaction was followed by his smirking smile. I had already learned to just laugh along at his jokes without admitting that I rarely understood the punch line. But in this case he hadn't been telling a joke. Why was it that the older girls that I admired were now chuckling along with him? The more uncomfortable I looked, the more he took delight in my bewilderment.

After a bit, Jess walked her horse up to me and tried to explain. "You know it's about . . . finishing," she offered, but this didn't help. I was ten years old and it was 1970. What did I know about orgasms? I hadn't even been taught the basics of sex ed.

Trying not to further expose my naiveté, I said, "Oh, okay," quietly and without conviction, which apparently came out sounding like a question. More laughter. I felt my face heat up with flushed embarrassment, adding a visible tip-off to an already humiliating situation. Now I was the butt of the joke for still not getting the joke.

Needing to pretend to be sexually savvy while protecting myself against my own vulnerability became a coping tactic. Strategies like this started impinging on my nervous system. The grooming process had officially begun.

CHAPTER 7

BELONGING

There is an innate fear that resides in all of us: the fear that we don't belong, that we aren't worthy as we are. As the months unfolded that school year, I became more and more identified with the culture surrounding horses and riding. It offered me a reassuring sense of acceptance. Learning the vocabulary related to horses added to the growing feeling that I was truly finding membership in the equine world.

I loved all the new words that high-stepped and pranced into my expanding lexicon. A simple word like "tack" stood for everything that could be put on a horse: pelham and snaffle bits, double-braided reins, browbands, throatlatches, and martingales. It also included the parts of the saddle: girths, pommels, cantles, and stirrups. Then there were the interesting words describing the body parts of a horse: withers, flanks, fetlocks, hocks, and chestnuts. And who knew that frogs were found on the bottom of hooves?

Given all of it, the colors of horses were my favorite expressions. Some sounded like ice cream flavors—strawberry roan, palomino, piebald, and pinto—and others sounded more like exotic paint colors: dapple gray, liver chestnut, and blood bay.

More specifically there was also the joy of learning the individual names of the horses and ponies that lived at our barn: Pilgrim and Jinx, Blythe Spirit and Little Elam, Trusty and Snaggletooth, Woodstock and Green Jeans, Sassafras and JJ, Levitation and Highlander, Brooks Brothers and Brother Brooks—the last two horses looked so much alike that only those from our stables could tell them apart.

All these new elite and exotic words represented the intoxicating immersion into the riding world in general and my life at Ivy Creek Stables in particular. I passionately wanted to be included in it. We all have an innate desire to feel valued and part of a community. We are, after all, social creatures at our core. Clarentine was the gatekeeper to this sense of connection I desperately wanted with horses and my emerging life at the stables. However, this need for belonging in us can also become the fertile ground for abuse.

It was spring and I had just turned eleven. "Hey, Blue Eyes, wanna show Smokey this weekend?"

"Yes!" I replied with enthusiasm, not even fully registering that Clarentine had just called me by a new nickname. Until that moment I had been wondering if he even remembered my actual name or just couldn't be bothered to use it. He had special monikers for others, too, so I heard this as a form of endearment. This and his invitation to compete in a show meant I had just officially been initiated into the group.

Everything at Ivy Creek Stables revolved around horse shows. Unlike other stables, Clarentine didn't charge fees for lessons. We could and did have unlimited access to riding at the stables without any financial cost, and we made the most of this seemingly "free rein" arrangement. When it came to entry fees for the shows themselves, this was determined on a case-by-case basis that was unclear to me back then. Sometimes my parents paid for my entry fees and sometimes he would cover them. My parents gave him the grazing rights to the fields that lay between my house and the stables. This arrangement wasn't overt to me and it took me even longer to realize that this may in fact have provided some invisible protection for me. This was just one of the many ways my privilege was hidden from me. One sure sign of having advantages is not needing to see them.

Regardless of whether the riders or he paid the entry fees, the accepted agreement was that he always pocketed whatever money was won. What his horses earned at horse shows made up an important part of his income. Pony classes offered the least in prize money, open jumping the most, but Clarentine strove to have at least one entry in every class so even we beginner riders could be valuable contributors. Showing was therefore the heartbeat of the stables. The training of the week culminated in traveling to a show every weekend from early spring through late fall.

For our part though, horse shows inspired our personal hopes and dreams. It's what we worked for, what motivated us. Each printed program that arrived in the mail was like anticipating Christmas. We would pore over the details of these folded paper brochures, noting the different competitions. What divisions or group of classes did they offer—Small Pony division? Green Hunter? Open Jumping? Were there any special classes listed that were one-offs like a Costume class, a Pair class, Gambler's Choice, Skyscraper? These programs told us how many ribbons they awarded per class. Was it judged to fourth place or all the way to sixth? Did they give out trophies? And most important of all, we would wonder which pony or horse Clarentine would assign us to. That first show he told me that I would be riding Smokey.

Now that my inaugural show was but a few days away, I dove into what I had been learning about the show preparations, which started with bathing, braiding, feeding, and mucking stalls for my pony, then included how to ready myself and pack for the full day at the show grounds. The rhythm of my life became structured around the cadence of these sensations: the sudsy feel of Ivory flakes while washing strong flanks and sinewy pony legs; the smell of Murphy Oil when applied to stirrup leathers or saddle flaps; the lushness of the soft rag I used to buff shoe polish into my boots, all tasks in preparation for the next big day. This routine would be my weekly ritual for many years to come.

Heading to the barn that first Saturday morning for the White Hall horse show, I carried my tack through the pre-dawn fields. The early April air was cool, although it already foreshadowed hints of the warmth to come. The stables were quiet except for the occasional profiled sound of snorting, the rooster crowing, a hoof stomping—all the more magnified in the muffled morning quiet that held the potential of the day. Other girls had already arrived, so there were movements afoot and a-hoof. I went to find Smokey and led him to the gathering of riders who were already loading horses into the van.

The van was an old meatpacking truck with metal siding. Clarentine had customized it by cutting out windows for airflow and attaching a drawbridge-like tailgate at the back. While other stables arrived in fancy trailers with separate stall compartments and roomy storage spaces, we would arrive in this metal contraption carrying up to six horses and two or three ponies packed together head-to-tail like sardines in a tin can.

Nowadays this horse van would undoubtedly be banned for lack of safety measures by animal protection agencies. For good reason. Regularly a horse would end up falling during transit and come out lame and/or spooked by the experience. Getting some horses to even load into the truck and into these cramped positions in the first place often became a protracted ordeal. But I hadn't had to witness that yet. On this particular morning, the loading and driving went smoothly. The show was a short drive away.

It used to be that many rural places hosted one of these annual shows in order to bring in revenue and provide entertainment for their communities. It was the town's big yearly event. Arriving at White Hall that first show day, I was greeted by a wild bevy of activities already underway. Vendors setting up stands, announcers testing sound systems over loudspeakers, cars and trailers rolling through the entrance gate, horses emerging everywhere as if by magic. Stands beginning to fill with spectators. Like a traveling circus that transforms a patch of previous quiet ground, it all seemed to spring into life at once.

After unloading and tying up our ponies, Kit and I walked over to the registration table to enter our classes and be assigned our numbers. Mist rose up from the dewy ground, the condensation giving way to the emerging warmth of the day. I would be riding in the small pony division, which was made up of three distinctly judged jumping competitions and a separate hack class on the flat—where riders would demonstrate all three gaits by riding around the ring at the same time. The accumulated points earned from these classes would determine which pony and rider would be named champion and reserve champion of that division. With our sights set high and holding what we hoped were our good luck numbers, Kit and I walked back to the van, taking in all the activities surrounding us.

We had been one of the first stables to arrive. Clarentine liked to have the pick of the best spots. Now I saw why. Our truck crouched in the rare bit of shade at one edge of the field in this otherwise open expanse. This area would provide some protection as the sun wore down the day.

"What are you standing around for?" Clarentine bellowed to me when I returned to the van. "You're up next!"

I hadn't been paying attention to the time as Kit and I meandered the grounds and now I realized I was in a crunch. I was gripped by a sudden panic that I was going to be late for my very first time in the ring.

"Oh no, I haven't braided my hair yet," I fretted. I needed to somehow contain my long strands under my riding helmet in a way that would look presentable to the judges. In the formal world of horse competitions, my own free-flowing mane would never do.

"Git over here. I'll do it for ya," came Clarentine's resounding voice. Without waiting for my response, he took out his tin of Copenhagen chewing tobacco and measured out a two-fingered pinch of chew. Placing it firmly in his mouth, he started to vigorously work his jaws. His cheeks bulged out on one side as the tobacco leaves turned into a pasty mush of dark cud leaking out around the edges of his lips. I'd seen him spit the repetitive excess into a Coke bottle, letting the dark, dribbled juice ooze down the inner glass sides and become a see-through collection of spit and gummy mash. But on this occasion, he spat into his hands instead. Rubbing his palms together and standing behind me, I suddenly recognized what was coming.

"Yuck!" I said in a half protest.

"Makes for better grip. Ya want it to hold, don't ya?" he countered. With open palms, now browned with juice, he began by firmly stroking my entire head of hair, flattening out all the wispy rogue ends like he would pet Major, his Doberman, back at the barn. It felt weird to have a grown man set to braid my hair, and with spit on his hands no less, but in this moment, it also felt gallant and attentive.

He spat again on each hand, reapplying his tobacco recipe for better tension, and began braiding. With thick fingers he divided up the three starting sections of hair—one near each of my temples, the other in the middle near the top of my head. I had always braided my own hair but didn't know how to do this more intricate weave. Turns out he was an adept French braider for someone with such heavily calloused, sausage-fingered work hands. I'd recently seen him braid a horse's tail in this same way. Stretching the sides tightly together, he crossed and wove the strands of my mink-brown mane, creating the resulting plaited section down the middle as he worked. Gathering a new strand of hair from each side of my scalp, this growing center braid flatly profiled the back of my head. At one particular twist he pulled painfully tight.

"Ouch!"

"Easy does it, filly," he soothed. At which point I raised my leg and playfully kicked back at him toward his shins. I couldn't fully connect to my insides at that moment, but I imagine it was part play and part annoyance. The wisp of mixed feelings was hard for me to identify, but the attention felt good. I felt cared for. This became my preferred narrative. Somewhere along the line these became the only feelings I chose to focus on. Splitting myself off became a defense against the rest.

"Whoa now, Nelly," he responded with a chuckle. Deliberately and carefully, he completed the task and tied off my braid with one of the small round rubber bands used for horses' manes.

"Can't say I never did nuthin' for ya," he joked.

I reached back to feel the firm pattern of it lying perfectly flat against my head. He was right—that chew-enhanced braid lasted me the whole show day.

The first class in my division was a warm-up jump class, so the course was shorter and the number of fences minimal, but it was my first time showing in front of an audience, and it seemed daunting. Clarentine stood at my side with me in the saddle, offering a few brief words of encouragement. "Ya got this."

Then Smokey and I entered the ring, trotted a small circle as I had been instructed, broke into a canter, and headed clockwise toward the first obstacle. It was a brush fence, and we ended up popping it. We made it over the fence, but we launched from too close in, so it was a jerky motion rather than the sought-after smooth jumping arc. Finding the right take-off spot was an art and the aim. Doing this consistently throughout the entire course was the goal for any hunter division. The judges were looking for an evenly paced and uniformly jumped ride. However, at that time, all I was focused on was getting over the fences and not "buying land" as we euphemistically called falling off.

The clapping I heard after my round with Smokey was reassuring and exhilarating. I patted his neck in gratitude as we slowed from a canter back down to a walk to exit the ring. He was tried and true. Nothing fancy, but steady and trustworthy. Just what I needed.

When all the entries had completed their rounds, there was a waiting period while the judge checked his notes and decided the winners. Kit and I, along with the other competitors, held the reins of our ponies outside the ring awaiting the verdict. "In first place, number 25," rang out the decision. Clarentine let out an audible whooping holler while Kit on foot trotted Misty into the middle of the ring. A blue ribbon was attached to the side of her bridle as she shook hands with the officials while the rest of us clapped and cheered loudly in the background.

"In second place . . ."

"In third place, number 14."

"Hey, that's you," someone indicated behind me. I had completely forgotten what number I was wearing on the back of my jacket. I jogged into the ring with Smokey trotting beside me to receive our yellow prize and accompanying envelope. Clarentine met us at the gate with his golden-toothed smile. He gave me a side-armed hug, relieved me of the envelope, and pointed me to the truck. I petted Smokey all the way back, untacked him, offered him water, and brushed his sweat-matted back. He was my hero. We were a team.

The ribbons we gathered throughout the day were displayed along a hay bale twine that Clarentine strung across the back of the truck. How thrilling to see my award added to the collective winnings of our stables. Here was confirmation that I was one of his riders. I belonged.

I couldn't help noticing during this first show the askance looks we received from other stables. There were those who rode for high-end outfits with grooms and personally embroidered blankets. In contrast, we rolled up in our converted meat truck carrying skinnier horses and disheveled equipment. We didn't fit the usual equestrian mold. We were the outsiders. But this only galvanized us more firmly as a group. We reveled in being the underdogs. This made the winning back then seem even sweeter. I didn't realize at the time that those looks from others weren't just about money.

At home that evening my parents were mildly impressed. "That's nice, honey." I found myself at a loss to put into words my myriad of feelings and how much riding already meant to me. The gap in their understanding of me seemed to be widening as the world of horses drew me further in.

Inspired by all the ribbons lined up on the side of the van, I proceeded to string a line across my own bedroom wall to proudly display this one cheery, yellow proof of my first horseback riding success. Later I would add red and blue ribbons and champion and reserve champion awards, making a colorful mosaic wallpaper. Show competitions became my elixir but also my kryptonite.

I didn't even notice the brown juice running from my hair as I took a shower later that night.

CHAPTER 8

HOUSE VS. HORSE

I couldn't have known then that Clarentine's dominance over his horses, and all of us, would have an indelible effect on how I came to relate to myself and others. He had an agenda, and we were merely the means to filling it. Decades into the future I would have to continue to untangle the web that these interactions had deeply stitched into me. It would show up in my marriage through my urge to control, my desire to get my needs met on my terms, and my hierarchical mindset. Clarentine was the epitome of what I would only much later be able to see as the same underpinning force behind our white patriarchal society. The conditioning of the general culture was seamlessly reinforcing what I was, in parallel, experiencing at those stables. And my craving to belong to it only magnified the fallout.

As I continued to unpack the source of my unconscious bullying of Mark in therapy now, the obvious connection was with what I had absorbed from Clarentine. However, with Gary's help, I began to see how my mother was simultaneously exerting her own version of domination and control on me in my home life as well. By now I had completed one year of middle school and had become one of Clarentine's riders.

The stables exemplified the antithesis of decorum in her view. So while I was starting to exercise my own need for independence, she was determined to shape me into her vision of how I should be behaving.

"You can't wear that. We're going to church and out for brunch afterward," she said with that tone of voice that indicated that I was about to flunk the "ladylike" test—again. My mom had always worried about what other people thought or might think. Here amidst the deep-rooted traditions of the South this anxiety became even more amplified in her.

"But I feel more comfortable in pants. I don't want to wear a dress," I countered, knowing that this was a fruitless battle but feeling compelled to push back anyway.

With a pursing of her lips and a flick of her wrist, she turned and walked away.

Sundays weren't the only time fraught with this conflict between us. What I wore, who I chose as friends, my use of grammar—they all became the battlegrounds of my youth. She wanted me to be feminine, well-mannered, deferential, and know how to properly use *who* and *whom*. I preferred wearing chaps and focusing on the meaning behind what I was saying, not the errors in my sentence structure.

There was that familiar nursery rhyme that she used to recite to me at night when I was little. "Girls are made of sugar and spice and all things nice, boys are made of snips and snails and puppy dog tails." I questioned even then, why did the boys get to have all the fun? Even before our move to Virginia she could never understand how I came home from school with my tights inevitably torn through at the knees. She couldn't relate to the fun I had skidding across gravel playgrounds while chasing or being chased by the boys during recess. She cringed when I brought home box turtles and frogs from the creek beyond our backyard. Perhaps my tomboy traits were my early attempts at differentiation, perhaps just my own inner countenance. Regardless, she and I were on different pages from the beginning. She took me on like a renovation project.

In addition, my mom was terrified of all things untamed—raucous laughter, loud voices, taking risks—horses!—and not being able to control her daughter. Doubling down on me was the only response to her anxiety that she knew. Power struggling was the constantly swirling river between our embankments.

At times, I railed against her attempts to shellac her expectations onto me. Defining myself as separate seemed like necessary self-preservation but left me not knowing who I was apart from this rebellion. At other times I was obedient to her wishes. I wanted her approval as much as I didn't want to be constrained by her, so surrendering to her control resulted in a temporary harmony between us. Compliance was reinforced.

I didn't understand the source of her demand for control at the time, but regardless it left me with these two choices: resist or capitulate. She was my reference point for both responses. I reflect now on how this added to my challenge of discovering my own separate personhood apart from her.

Back to our frequently repeated Sunday dramas, my dad, having heard us bickering about my attire, entered the scene with his own typecast response.

"You are upsetting your mother," he'd calmly but declaratively chime in. He was always the pacifying arbitrator in our clashes. While my mother was controlling and anxious, my dad was even-tempered, passive, and a quintessential "conflict avoider," a fitting label I learned about only much later when I entered the world of psychology. He responded to her anxious need for control by trying to preemptively placate her. If she was content, then we all were, went his faulty logic. He tried to get my brother and me to buy into the same strategy.

"Just do what she asks" became my dad's mantra because when she didn't get her way, there was a price to pay. She would implode with angry outbursts followed by a withdrawal into a chilling silence that could blow a frigid wind through the house for days. Then at an undetermined time, there would come a break in the emotional weather, and suddenly everything was somehow forgotten. Life resumed as if nothing had happened. There was an empty and unsatisfying sense of relief for all of us when we temporarily landed at this point in the cycle.

When I wasn't railing against the injustice of this situation, I, too, learned to soothe and tiptoe around her moods. It meant that most issues and conflicts remained unacknowledged and unresolved. No wonder that life at the barn seemed to offer something compelling and attractive. And yet, in retrospect, it was also familiar for me to dance around a commanding personality. Out of necessity I was already adept at that.

On one particular Sunday that stands out in my memory, I was still hearing my mother's criticism in my head as I pouted my way back to my room to put on something "acceptable." I didn't want to be shown off like a souvenir, paraded out to those we'd run into at the University Baptist Church for Sunday service or during brunch in our small town afterward.

It strikes me as ironic that I detested this but didn't mind the thought of being trotted out on a horse in a ring wearing the also strictly required riding attire. There were constrictions everywhere I turned, but the world atop a pony was so much more appealing. And being on show was vastly different when you were the one holding the reins. At least I told myself I was holding the reins back then.

At church, the four of us sat in a middle row on the hard, wooden-backed pew, hands folded, our movements monitored by sideways looks from Mom. I fantasized that our warm pastor somehow saw all this and silently validated my predicament even though he was helpless to intercede. However, in reality my mother was savvier than this. She knew how to photoshop a living family portrait for others.

Later that morning at the stodgy country club she oozed tension over brunch while we ate eggs Benedict and lox, creamy cheese grits, and slices of Virginia baked ham topped off with Southern pecan pie. But others who knew her less well only saw her ability to work a room, be polite, and offer her social graces.

I longed to be seen and accepted by her, and yet I was repelled by the constrictions that she was invisibly bound by. I felt the need to distance myself from her in order to hold onto my budding self. All this only served to plunge me headlong and headstrong into life at the barn.

I ran in the front door following brunch that afternoon, like every afternoon, and quickly replaced the tights with cut-off shorts, traded in my feminine dress for a grubby T-shirt, grabbed my chaps, and headed for the barn. I loved it when I could cast off my good girl outfit in exchange for my comfy cowgirl one. My sense of freedom seemed to increase in proportion to the exchanged clothing and my proximity to the barn. The house was my mom's domain; the barn was mine.

At the barn I could wear whatever I wanted—and was expected to get dirty doing it. I would sometimes accumulate so much brown dust from the ring sticking to my sweat that I had a fried chicken look by the end of the day. I reveled in the line I'd discover when changing clothes, that place where dirt pushed right up against and defined exactly where it met my unexposed, contrasting pale skin.

There was also the manure that clung to my well-worn Docksiders, the itchy hay captured in my mousey brown hair, and the general barn grime under my fingernails. These were all proof of a hard day's work in the outdoors, the world beyond the confines of a pristine, magazine-decorated home. The world that offered something more than how girls "should" be.

The midday heat was thick and clawing that afternoon, but I barely noticed. I had the rest of the day to languish at the barn around the horses with my horsey friends. It would be too hot to ride during the peak of this sizzling day, but hanging out with the others and Clarentine would nourish the sense of belonging I craved.

By the time I got there, many girls were already lounging under the large dogwood tree near the ring that provided precious shade. Some were slumped at the picnic table while others melted into cast-iron chairs and onto two chain-sawed tree stumps set out as makeshift seats for just such a gathering. Kit and I were peers, then there were those who were older by only a handful of years, and a few who were young, single-parent moms who came to the barn with their own young daughters. Clarentine's ace riders, the ones who were jumping, training, and winning at the highest level, occupied the inner circle here at the barn. I looked up to them, wanted to be like them, longed to ride as they could. Overall, we were a motley collection made up of girl fillies and young mares—never colts.

"Had to go to church again, eh?" one teased. I was envious of the lack of restrictions many of them had in their lives. I hobbled together a brief response as I claimed a seat on one of the empty stumps but felt again how my family's expectations cost me precious time at the barn. I came to learn later that for different reasons we were all attempting to avoid something at home that we hoped to find here.

The chitchat became coded as it sometimes did. I wasn't able to follow all the references and inside jokes. Then Clarentine suddenly appeared from around the corner of the barn carrying a large watermelon. The oppressive heat that was expressing itself in everyone's slumped posture now made us all sit up in anticipation of this cooling antidote.

"Today's hotter than a mad hen," he announced while taking out the large buck knife that he always kept sheathed to his side. Inexplicably, he always referred to this knife as his "wife." Never having married, this declaration of relationship was an odd commitment, but that knife was always with him.

With this wife blade, he began cutting into the reptilian-designed rind, which revealed its oozing red meat dotted with methodically spaced black seeds. We all watched as he halved, then quartered, then triangled our separate pieces, handing them out as the pink liquid rolled down his hands and blond, hairy, tanned arms. We each waited patiently for our turn, all of us secretly registering the hierarchy this expressed. There were hidden variables to this equation that I didn't understand at the time. It wasn't until later that I realized the price exacted, the cost incurred for moving up in this determination of status.

Meanwhile, I was still trying to understand my place here at the barn and how the ordering worked. It may have been us against them outside of the barn, but inside, there was a competitive undercurrent. At eleven, I was one of the last to receive a piece, but the sequence wasn't necessarily determined by age.

I watched as the older girls I admired chomped into their watermelon slices, letting the juice flow over their chins and necks with each bite. Never would this abandon be allowed at my house, I thought to myself. But then, my family would never even be eating outside, without napkins, without plates and utensils, without our Emily Post manners.

Gleefully following their lead, I bit into my wedge, mimicking the carefreeness of letting the sticky nectar roll down my own face and forearms. We shared smiles and laughs at the pure messiness of this unfettered eating. With his own man-sized piece in hand, Clarentine slurped and sucked with conspicuously loud delight. Then he reared back his head and with an *oomph* and a *thwaap* he shot out a dark oval seed from his mouth. It flew through the fence boards and landed an impressive distance far inside the dry, dusty ring.

"Whoa!" some of us said in unison.

"How did you do that?"

"Show us!"

He demonstrated how to curl our tongues like Fruit Roll-Ups around these little individual projectiles, draw in a deep breath, and sharply exhale with added upper body momentum to catapult the little seed into an arcing flight path of our own making. Quickly this practice was transformed into a raucous seed-spitting contest, each of us slurping up the fruity freshness and spitting out the black nuggets, measuring our success amidst friendly debate and laughter. With sticky chins and even stickier hands we had all momentarily forgotten the oppressive heat.

I relished leaving behind the rigidity of tights and good girl grooming in order to be sitting here in my comfortable cut-off shorts among these girls who were becoming my friends. I reveled in it all—tasting the juicy fruit, spitting seeds, getting dirty.

What wasn't apparent to me then is that rebellion against isn't the same thing as freedom. It is still being chained to an external point of reference. Defining myself as not my mother was not the same as discovering who I was independent of my reaction to and resistance against her. There is no real choice inherent in "not that." Her rigidity and my defiance of it was careening me into another kind of danger.

CHAPTER 9

LIKE MY MOTHER

"You're just like your mother." Gary started a session with what felt like a karate kick to my solar plexus. I had been out of the house for a month by then and was desperately working to figure out how I had managed to blow up my marriage. I was still compelled to attack this problem as if it could be solved by a secret missing formula.

He paused, then added, "Like her, you expect Mark to take care of your anxiety and you blame him if he doesn't."

"Wait, I am not anxious," I defensively blurted out, hearing the disdain in my voice at being compared to her. "Look at my mother if you want to see an example of anxiety. She can't tolerate anything or anyone that causes her to feel uncomfortable." I emphasized this point with a scornful tone. I never wanted to feel consumed by her fear of life, so I rebelled by taking risks, refusing to follow the agenda she set for me and fighting the windmill battles that distanced me from being likened to her. That made me not like her, right? At least that is the story I told myself.

It was true that being out of the house had set off a buzzing beehive that constantly reverberated throughout my body. I couldn't settle down my nervous system. I was on continual vibrate mode with no way to swipe it off. But I still wanted to downplay this current evidence of my anxiety, not to mention my denial of all the other non-circumstantial ways that an undercurrent of angst shadowed me.

"Maybe it takes a different form than hers, but you aren't any less anxious than she is," Gary continued. "You deny these feelings and therefore obscure the truth to yourself." As my therapist, Gary's job was to point out the incongruities between what I wanted to believe about myself and the reality of me, as shown through my actions. He always did have a picture window view of my insides, and the exposure often felt eviscerating. We all want to be seen and loved for who we are, and yet at the same time we fear being abandoned if our deepest selves are revealed. Our ego's misplaced mission then becomes self-preservation by avoiding vulnerability at all costs.

Being seen by Gary in this moment was causing my ego to wince under the onslaught that he might be right—I might be like my mother. She was always wigged out by whatever situation or outcome she couldn't control. *Is that really true of me, too? Have I been avoiding seeing the ways that I'm also anxious in order to push away how we are similar? Damn, didn't I just do this? Ugh!*

My mother would deny and gaslight anyone who noticed her level of stress. Then she would blame them for having those distressing feelings. A regular exchange between us would go something like, "Mom, I can tell that you are anxious, but it's going to be okay."

"I am NOT anxious. How can you even say that?" was her knee-jerk response, a far cry from validating my reality. As kids, when our experience of what is happening isn't accurately reflected back, it generates self-doubt and anxiety. For me the resulting internal dialogue became something to the effect of, *I'm seeing all the signs of my mom being stressed out, but she's denying this. If that's not what's going on, then what is? Is it my fault? Am I responsible for her feelings?* Children aren't equipped with a lens that can take in the full picture. It's hard enough for adults to do. Thus the tendency is to internalize some form of self-blame for somehow not being enough.

As my conversation with Gary continued to dig into this, I realized that her anxiety wasn't actually the main problem—it was that she could never own it. If my mother had only been able to admit it. If only she had softened in this way. If she could have said, "I am so on edge today. I am worried about . . ." Fill in the blank—it could have been the holiday dinner she was hosting or that she was running late for an appointment. If only she could have said, "I see that this anxiety is spilling out onto you. I am sorry you take the brunt of this. This is my problem, not yours."

Wow! Not only would this have confirmed my experience, but then I could have relaxed and better trusted that she was interested in taking care of her side of the fence and not just dumping it on me to solve and feel responsible for.

Gary, the stark truth-teller, added, "Look, we learn from the modeling we received. When your mom was anxious, she tried to control her surroundings and everyone in it. You act on your anxiety in similarly aggressive ways. Whatever we disown in ourselves, we end up projecting onto others. These become the acts of violence that cause harm."

When I could slow it down to look at what Gary was saying, I was aghast at the truth of it. It was easy to be interested in Mark's needs—when those happened to line up with my own. But when they didn't, I could become judgmental, controlling, and manipulative in order to get the outcome I wanted—fueled by my own anxiety. Taking stock, I realized that I regularly prioritized my own comfort at his expense. Similar to how I saw my mother treat my dad, which was hard to witness, these were indeed forms of aggressive behavior. I could no longer deny the high cost all this had been having on my own marriage.

I had to admit that I AM like my mother! Not only did I have to accept that I had adopted her similar coping mechanisms, but I also had to own that I had recreated a marriage not unlike my parents'. And I expected Mark to play along with this arrangement—just as I saw my father defer to my mom in order to avoid conflict. I'd spent my entire life trying to not be like her when, ironically, my reactivity and denial ended up duplicating her to a tee! This was a hard wedge of truth to swallow.

I left this session feeling raw and yet somehow also oddly relieved. In-depth therapy can feel like a Rolfing massage. It painfully pries apart the emotional myofascial muscles that have long since become unhealthfully glued together. Untangling the ways that the influences in our lives become deeply woven into our tissue layers allows for a new freedom of movement. As a result I felt sore but also more open.

CHAPTER 10

MATERNAL FRACTURING

We are all unwitting archivists of our ancestral lineage. This can translate into both a source of our resilience and our Achilles' heel. Being able to identify what we have emotionally inherited, the strengths as well as the latent traumas, helps us see the forces at work within us.

Week by week with Gary's help I attempted to cut deeper into these layers of my own geology, probing into how the parenting I received not only set me up for what happened to me at the barn but also impacted the way I was now approaching my marriage and motherhood. With my relationship with my husband in crisis, I was motivated to continue to excavate all the hidden forces that had influenced my development as a person and the burdens I was now exerting on my loved ones as a result.

Because we embody the culmination of all that has come before, we become the receptacles of both what is consciously passed down and what is kept hidden. However, secrets exert the greatest impact on our lives because it is more difficult to address the invisible.

Around the time that we first moved to Virginia, my aunt told me one such family secret that rattled me to my core. From then on I was stunned that this deeply unsettling chapter in our family legacy was only ever mentioned in rare private whispers and, like unwelcome cobwebs, quickly whisked away. Now back in the throes of therapy, I knew that my grandmother's tragic story held another piece of the puzzle for understanding the inherited forces continuing to partition off parts of me.

I tried to envision that terrible day, that I was just now hearing about, that changed everything for my maternal grandmother, Bessie. This scene opens with her sitting beside the bed of her own dying mother. She would have been in her early thirties then, a young mother at the time, emotionally squeezed between raising her own young daughters and simultaneously holding vigil through the impending death of her mother. I conjure up a picture of Bessie tenderly holding this old woman's shriveled hand, her own shoulders drooping under the grief-laden weight of this final farewell period with the family matriarch.

"I need to tell you something before I die, something that I've never told you before now," this old woman likely began. There might have followed a pause for her to inhale a ragged breath in order to proceed. Through cracked lips she then managed to eke out the truth. "I took you from your own family when you were very little and raised you as if you were my own daughter."

I imagined my grandmother thinking, *What?! I was kid-napped!* This long-held secret must have suddenly exploded into a deafening silence. In that one horrendous moment, flash frozen by what she had just been told, my grandmother must have struggled mightily to absorb the implications of this newly revealed confession, and I think about what she likely thought: *Could this be true? Was I really abducted as a child? Taken from my birth family? By the very person I've called "Mother" for my entire lifetime?*

Just as quickly the woman lying on her deathbed defended her actions with justifications that might have sounded something like: "You must understand, I wasn't able to have children of my own. I believe God brought you and me together so that I could finally be a parent. Besides, it wasn't fair that the neighbor woman was blessed with so many children. I didn't think that she would miss you, her youngest. One less mouth to feed."

Some version of this awful story provided the justifications that she used to excuse her criminal actions and keep the baying wolves of guilt at a distance. It helped her sleep at night through all those years of raising a kidnapped girl as her own daughter.

As my aunt recounted to me, both families were immigrants from Denmark working homesteading land in rural Pennsylvania in the waning years of the 1890s. This woman had made friends with the family living on the next farm over. They were neighbors during a time when having community meant surviving together through harsh winters and scarce summer crops. Perhaps the kidnapping wasn't premeditated from the start, but when she, childless, became attached to the youngest, a devious plan must have begun to form.

I conjure in my mind a picture of an otherwise ordinary sunny day when all the older siblings were playing in the rural fields beyond their modest farmhouse. I imagine the kidnapper offered to keep an eye on young Bessie as she had done before. But on this day when no one was watching, she seized her opportunity and quietly picked up the young girl and walked unnoticed out of the yard, never to look back. Together with her husband, they made a speedy escape via a train heading further into the Midwest.

In those days, there was no coordinated way to locate missing children. There were no Amber Alerts buzzing on cell phones, no national databases to track information. The FBI was yet to exist. And besides, the police wouldn't be that concerned about a new immigrant family's pleas anyway. This meant that a couple, carrying a kidnapped child and pretending she was their own, could travel by train across state lines into Illinois, the equivalent of a world away, and disappear for a lifetime. They started again as a false family of three, rewriting history and never being held accountable for this unfathomable crime.

Was this woman's ability to rationalize so perfected that she never thought about the life she stole? Did she have no remorse while cooking the child's dinner each evening or tucking her into bed? Did she never consider the wailing grief of a mother whose child had vanished that fateful afternoon? Or of the years spent trying to find her? Of the guilt and pain of a maternal loss that never abates?

And what about the husband of the kidnapper? Did he try to stop his wife when she first brought up the heinous idea? Or did he rationalize that this was what would make her happy, solve her childless sadness, and so make it all somehow okay? That child never had a chance to ask him. He was complicit in this crime but took it to his earlier grave.

What finally motivated this bedside confession? Why then? The abductor might have told herself that she wanted her daughter to know the truth before she died. However, she could have made amends years earlier if it was really about apologizing for her actions. No, this was purely self-serving. She needed to relieve her own guilty conscience. She wanted to be released from the dark secret she had stored away. She wanted to save her own soul. Put simply, being an avidly Christian woman, I imagine she feared going to Hell. Confessing before her death would be her final act of repentance and hopeful redemption.

I wonder what was happening to Bessie's insides when she found out this grisly truth—that her whole life had been built on a terrible lie. How could she even ingest a confession that shattered her whole world?

At some visceral level, our bodies know the truth, but secrets are like an invisible force field, undetectable but well-positioned to block our understanding. As a young child, my grandmother must have had some recessed memory like leftover trinkets from a different life. A vague recollection of the familiar smell of another woman. The feel of different arms holding her. The sounds of laughter and playful footsteps from a house full of children. Had she ever asked about these memories? If so, she would have been told that she had gotten it all wrong. Protecting this secret would require denying young Bessie's felt experience over and over again. Reality for her had been obliterated from the beginning.

A masquerading mother robbed this child first of her birth family and the life she was meant to live. Then she robbed her of the truth. Then on her deathbed she robbed any possibility of a genuine response to this seismic injury. As the only mother Bessie knew, she also loved this woman and felt indebted to her. And now she was dying. The waves of conflicting emotions must have been deeply unsettling.

Dear Grandmother, what did you do and say in that moment to this woman who had long ago kidnapped you and for whom you were now tenderly caring? What could you say? You'd been trained to subdue your emotions, your intuition, your authentic reactions. You were programmed to be dutiful, subservient. You were up against so many obstacles to finding your voice. You were female at the turn of the twentieth century, stoically Danish, taught scripture about obeying one's parents, and drilled to just be grateful for what you had—all forms of conditioned silencing. Any impulse to shout out in anger, keen with grief, lash out at your abductor, stand up and leave . . . likely dissipated before having gained any traction.

Also during this particular day of reckoning, the sheer shock of the truth must have been too much to take in. How does one attempt to reconcile one's life story when a new fact reduces it to fiction? We aren't wired for such devastating news. Denial and shock are the mechanisms that save us from imploding upon impact. So perhaps instead my grandmother sat in a state of paralysis. Perhaps she reflexively forgave her without digestion. Perhaps Bessie excused herself to go sit in the bathroom and weep softly for the life taken from her. Maybe she did all of the above.

What I do know is that my grandmother buried her soon afterward, along with many unanswered questions. She must have wondered, *Where does my biological mom live? What's happened to her and the rest of my family? Are they still alive? Did they search for me? Did they grieve for me? Have they forgotten about me by now? What about my siblings?*

Following up on a few clues, my grandmother, Bessie, did eventually go in search of her biological family. She managed to locate an address and, getting behind the wheel, drove alone toward the possibility of a reunion. As I was told, Bessie slowed down as she neared the house, a house that in a parallel universe would have been her own. There in front was an old woman hanging laundry on the clothesline. The resemblance of her features was mirrored in Bessie's own face. I imagine that my grandmother had debated with herself during this drive about whether she would stop and introduce herself to this woman who was her real mother or keep driving by. Could she bring herself to meet her in that moment?

The answer turned out to be "no." That was too great a chasm of grief and loss for my grandmother to bridge. Stepping into pain and vulnerability requires enormous courage. She didn't trust that it also held the potential for healing and reconciliation. I sometimes wonder how my family legacy might have been altered if she could have met that moment differently.

Did my grandmother later regret that she missed this opportunity? There was never a second chance. The mother she never knew died soon afterward. Although she did later experience a long overdue reunion with her surviving older siblings, it was always awkwardly apparent that they had lived a life that didn't include her.

My grandmother died soon before I was born, and my own mother rarely spoke about her. It appears that they shared the same coping mastery of disassociating from upsetting feelings. Reconciling the truth of our lives takes such fortitude. My mother had learned from her mother that this was an unsafe path to tread. This avoidance of pain and difficult feelings has become encoded throughout my maternal lineage.

Not being able to address our own hurts means we inevitably download them onto ourselves and others. My grandmother raised my mother through her unhealed wounds. Now, here was my mother channeling onto me an accumulation of compartmentalized pain and grief. As a result, I experienced my relationship with my mom regularly go up in flames or lead to a protracted blizzard unless I, too, cut myself off from my emotions and experiences.

Disowning our feelings distances us from intimacy with others. We forfeit the chance of working through differences and discovering the deeper understanding and compassion that exists between human hearts. Instead, my maternal ancestry perpetuated a succession of emotional cleaving. A lineage of fractured selves demands the same in return. The homing device that might have brought my mom and me into a shared orbit had long ago been disabled.

CHAPTER 11

SELF-SPLINTERING

L ooking back, I can see examples of how I, too, became adept at this same coping strategy. It was the second summer since I'd moved as a young girl to the rural part of Charlottesville and an afternoon that Clarentine called a "fried egg day" because the oven-like temperatures could literally cook an egg on the pavement. Even though I was well-heeled into my daily routine at the barn, the intrusive summer heat still took some getting used to.

"Come on, let's run up to the store. I need to git a few things. It'll be quick." Thinking that a cold drink would taste delicious in the face of that plastering humidity, I eagerly jumped into the truck with Clarentine, looking forward to the ride.

The town of Ivy was just down the road "a piece" and, like many rural dots on the map, barely registered as a legitimate town. It consisted of a locally owned gas station, a shed-sized post office, and a mercantile general store. These modest wayside services however were a rare oasis along this quiet stretch of road midway between Charlottesville to the east and Crozet to the west. For locals and travelers alike, the Ivy Store sold a hodgepodge of quick in and out items—convenient canned foods and basic staples and snacks, along with fishing bait, flashlights, and motor oil. It was also the source of news and local gossip, a gathering place to "shoot the shit."

Outside there was always a congregation of mongrel dogs. The flea-bitten and mangy ones angled for handouts while the others patiently awaited their owners' reemergence from within. All were preoccupied with scratching themselves while sprawling lazily on the hot, dusty ground.

The wooden porch steps themselves were rubbed down to a worn concave polish from years of repetitive use. Heavy, steel-toed work boots, gum-soled muck boots, knee-high riding boots, and most everything in between crossed those steps.

The screened porch door announced our entrance and someone else's exit with a sharp clap against the side doorframe jamb like a dutiful sentry. Inside, the hand-laid floorboards between half-wall aisles were akin to the steps, shiny with wear. During the sweltering deep Virginia summer, the fans, strategically placed, spun full blast with a steady, rhythmic thrumming, and still there was little respite inside from the clinging heat.

Long past their prime, amber-colored flypaper strips hung from parts of the ceiling. Once presumably sticky, they now only passively displayed their captured trophies in the form of leggy, black miniature carcasses. Meanwhile, plenty of other flies, both dead and alive, congregated on the windowsills, a similar scene to that of the tack room back at the barn.

Clarentine and I—he the hulking man, and me the spindly-limbed eleven-year-old—went our separate ways upon entering the familiar store. I roamed the middle aisle and found my favorite Twinkies. Then in pursuit of something to drink, I headed to the deep refrigerator box that hunched at the back of the store. The horizontal lid sleepily pulled up as it hinged open. The rush of arctic air made me linger a bit longer for the refreshing moment it offered while I grabbed a cold Mountain Dew from the line of soft drinks nestled up next to the night crawlers. Holding my bounty, I let the heavy lid sink back down with a suctioned close.

Clarentine was garnering his own collection of miscellaneous items: a box of nails to fix a fence and a small bag of scratch feed to tide over the chickens, along with a loaf of bread, a carton of milk, a can of Copenhagen chewing tobacco, and a tall glass bottle of Coke. Cradling our individually gathered items, we met back at the front of the store.

"What ya hearing about Randy's place up for sale?" Clarentine asked the gnarled man standing behind the old, ornate cash register.

"Ain't no one with a right mind's goin' throw away good cash on that farm."

"Yeah, floods every time it even thinks about raining."

"And for what they asking!"

"Never know, there's a sucker born every minute," Clarentine concluded with what I was coming to recognize as his typically cynical summation.

"Today, got money burning a hole in my pocket," he stated while gesturing for me to put my soda and snack on the counter along with his items. This same surface was crowded with gallon-sized mason jar specimens that looked like mad scientist experiments. These displayed not only gigantic dill pickles but also the delicacies of the South—pickled pigs' feet, pigs' ears, and mountain oysters—all floating in discolored, cloudy liquids in large separate glass containers. Meanwhile, the hefty brass cash register took no mind as it assertively dinged out each purchase.

When we got back to the truck, Clarentine used his knife and a corner edge of the cab to knock off the bottle cap and pour out much of the soda onto the ground. At first I didn't understand why he would be emptying out the perfectly good cola that he had just purchased. I realized the answer to this when he grabbed his stashed bottle of Old Crow bourbon from beneath the driver's seat. I watched as Clarentine twisted off the bourbon cap and carefully poured a narrow stream of the amber liquid straight into the thin-necked bottle of remaining Coke. From the passenger seat I observed how he mixed this concoction with a surgeon's precision. This was the first time I had witnessed this particular ritual up close. At the barn I had only seen his drink already in hand. Like everything else I was becoming inured to the ubiquitous presence of alcohol too.

During this interlude something on the cab floor flashed in my periphery. Leaning forward slightly, I could see a long metal nose poking out from under the seat. Clarentine saw my focus and pushed the gun back out of view. I knew he owned guns, including a rifle that he used for target practice, but I hadn't until then quite connected that he always had a weapon close at hand—even during a short trip to the store and back. In this case it was a pistol under the truck seat when he was behind the wheel.

The story I told myself was that this proved that he could protect me. Right? Any discomfort I might have felt was already being relegated to those secreted places inside myself so that I could construct a more bearable narrative. As time went by, I grew more skillful at omitting these incongruences. In fact, this kind of disconnect and self-deception on my part seemed almost like an innate ability. Turns out I did come from a long line of ancestors who were adept at fragmenting away difficult emotions and terrible truths while simultaneously presenting something entirely different to the external world.

As we drove back to the barn, I had no way of knowing then that that same gun, always lying in wait like a coiled rattler camouflaged under a rock, would one day become a murder weapon.

CHAPTER 12

THE EXTRACTION

While the barn offered me an illusion of freedom to explore my unbridled self, connect with horses, and get a break from my mother's controlling ways, it was at the expense of not only being subjected to the sexual grooming but also included the witnessing of physical violence that infused this environment. The aggression and domination that we girls at the stables were all exposed to became normalized in my narrative over time.

I can trace the beginning of this desensitization process to a subtle example that occurred later that same summer when I was eleven. A few of us were standing around the tack room listening to the country music that continuously emanated from the radio station where the dial was permanently set.

"Here, come take a look," Clarentine said, motioning us closer. He proceeded to display a lump located on the underside of his arm. This odd bulge had seemingly appeared overnight.

"What is that?" I asked with part intrigue, part revulsion.

Not answering my question, he asked instead, "Wanna touch it?"

"Eww, no," I said.

"C'mon, feel right here," he urged, and before I could step away, he grabbed my hand and guided my fingers to roll over this mysterious, hard bump.

I found myself momentarily fascinated. He was right. It was strangely firm to the touch, lying just inside his upper arm. It was oddly well-defined, capsule-like in shape and size.

"Shouldn't you see a doctor or something?" I ventured.

"Why, I never met a doc with a lick-a-sense." His aversion and disregard for the medical profession was a rant I had heard before.

Over the next few days, he was thoroughly preoccupied with this physical anomaly. He showed it to all who came to the barn and fiddled with it like a worry stone while he talked.

One morning later that week, I arrived early at the barn and found him smiling like a cat with a mouse's tail in his mouth. He couldn't wait to show me his arm. The place where the object had been lodged was now lying flat again. It was obvious he had cut into the protruding area of the bump.

"I used my 'wife' to cut it out," he beamed, referencing the large bowie knife that was never far from his side. Pulling out the impressive blade, he demonstrated how he had taken the pointy end of this hefty metal, made for much cruder jobs, and used the very tip to break into his skin at the edge of this mysterious mound. He illustrated with gestures how he carved into his own flesh, wedging the blade tip beneath the alien object, and leveraged it enough to pop it out. He said it emerged like a cork from a bottle, sprung out wholly intact.

"Lookie here," he bragged. And reaching into his pocket, he opened his fisted hand. There in the middle of his palm was a bullet!

He said he had been speculating that it was the same one he had been shot with some decades earlier. This extraction now confirmed his suspicions. We had all heard his story of having gotten into a fight in the neck of the woods where he grew up. As he recounted it, this conflict involved a fight over a girl that had ended in gunshots. He had killed the other man in the process. He had also been hit at the time but hadn't bothered to get the bullet removed.

It was common knowledge that he had killed not one but two men in his past and had spent time in prison for this second incident. It sounds strange in hindsight that these facts were so publicly known and verifiable and yet everyone's response was so ho-hum. Hard to understand how the adults were allowing their young girls to participate in this "stable" environment that was anything but stable. The ability to make a questionable reality acceptable is still stunning. However, denial is our strongest coping mechanism—a fact that I would come to know for myself all too well.

Clarentine, still holding the piece of ammunition in his palm, continued to speculate out loud. "Must of made its way clear cross my body from here where I was shot . . ."—he indicated by pointing first to a mark on his left side near his ribs, then tracing the conjectured path it must have taken to migrate fully across his upper chest—"until it found its way to just here," he concluded, touching the exact spot where he had removed the bullet from his inner arm.

This incident certainly fit neatly into what I already knew about him. I knew that he owned guns and rifles. I had seen him shrug off pain that would have toppled someone else. I knew that he would not have sought out medical attention, nor did they necessarily have this resource available where he grew up.

Was he thrilled that it was finally out, this chapter completed? Did he feel smug knowing that he had outlived the other man? Was he bolstered by being able to impress us with this story? I sensed that it was all of the above.

Unfortunately, extracting a bullet from his body didn't scare me away—just the opposite. His rogue character and Wild West bravado appealed to my idealistic girl self. Here was proof that things like this didn't just happen in the movies. They were happening right now in my own life to my riding instructor. Clarentine had participated in two deadly conflicts and come out as the sole survivor each time.

Turns out he could pull a bullet from his own body as easily as he could put one into another. I couldn't know then that this would foreshadow another fatal altercation to come, but in the meantime day by day and unbeknownst to me, I was being assimilated into his culture of violence.

Soon after coming into contact with Clarentine's past through the extracted bullet, we girls witnessed a scary brawl. In a distorted way it served to further bind me to him.

The threat drove up the driveway late one Sunday afternoon. This stranger emerged from his beater car with an exaggerated slam of the door. He looked to be in his twenties and was thin as a fence rail, facially gaunt with stringy long hair and darting wild eyes. It was known in the community that anyone could rent horses at Ivy Creek Stables. It was another way that Clarentine generated income. So we riders regularly tacked up horses for all kinds of people that came for trail riding. We were already gearing up to find him a horse, so it was jarring when he started shouting, "Get me a goddamn horse, now!"

As we stood stunned by this unexpected ranting, his voice grew even louder. "Don't you see that I am here to ride, dammit!"

Kit was the first to find her feet and ran to alert Clarentine, who was shoeing a horse near the upper barn. But having heard the commotion, he was already striding his way toward us. In his deep, I-mean-business voice, he told the man to leave—immediately. The man responded with a belligerent, "You can't make me. This here's a free country." We all scrambled backward as the space between the two men narrowed and began to heat up. Words slingshot back and forth. Then suddenly the intruder was holding an open switchblade that must have been previously concealed in his pocket.

He lunged for Clarentine, who dodged the knife but was able to catch hold of his wrist in the process. Tumbling to the ground in wrestling style, they scuffled against the hard-packed dirt in a mini-cyclone of whirling boots, jeans, and limbs.

I exchanged furtive glances with the other girls gathered nearby. None of us knew what we should be doing. It was horrifying and paralyzing and weirdly hypnotizing in the same breath. The fight then took a decisive turn. Clarentine managed in one motion to twist the blade out of his attacker's hand, wrench his arm behind his back, and pin his cheek flat against the ground. The other man's movements were still spastic but slowing.

"I'll let ya up when ya agree to leave," Clarentine asserted. The man took a pause and conceded with a nod. This was enough to satisfy Clarentine into releasing his restraint. The man slowly kneeled his way up to standing.

"And ya betta never set foot here again or ya will regret it. Ya hear me!"

Without another word or a look back, the man limped to his car and drove off.

In that moment, rather than being alarmed by the fight I had just witnessed, I felt a wave of gratitude for having just been protected. That day proved that the world of outsiders could clearly be a scary place. I was on the cusp of becoming conscious of how powerless I was in the scheme of things. Clarentine was strong, intimidating, afraid of nothing and no one. Wasn't being taken care of by a powerful man the next best thing to holding that power oneself? Looking back, it was so ironic that I was developing a narrative about Clarentine as a means of feeling more secure when I was anything but safe in his presence. Admiration isn't always discerning.

CHAPTER 13

THE PROGRESSION OF AGGRESSION

Time galloped by. Thoroughly enamored with horses, I continued to ride every day and was regularly winning ribbons and money for Clarentine. I was living what seemed to me an unrestrained life. I spent as much unsupervised time at the barn as I wanted. I came and went as I pleased. However, at the same time that I saw Clarentine as my mentor, examples of his uncurbed aggression also started to accumulate piecemeal. The unpredictable bouts of rage that he could and would fly into began adding a simmering fear to my admiration. Like Jekyll turned Hyde, these episodes of violent anger and the ever-looming possibility of brutality garnered a level of dread and obedience in all of us—the horses too.

One example of this progressive exposure to violence and my own responding disconnect happened the day Clarentine told me to go wrangle up Dooner and meet him under the oak trees. He was a gorgeous blood bay colt with a beautiful blaze running slightly askew down his forehead. His nickname around the barn was "Lance Romance" because his sweet disposition charmed everyone. I was first introduced to him the morning after his birth a year and a half previously when he was just learning to stand on new stilted legs.

With a rope lead line attached to his halter, I walked him over to the shaded area where Clarentine usually did his outdoor shoeing. While in transit it finally clicked that instead of this being a spring shoeing day, it might be a gelding day. I knew that most colts wouldn't be left to mature into stallions because they would become so difficult to handle. Having one at our stables was enough, but it was still a mystery to me what this process entailed. When our cocker spaniel returned from being neutered at the vet, I hadn't asked any questions. In my naiveté I couldn't (or didn't want to) grasp what this now might mean for this young horse, but it didn't sound good.

When I arrived with Dooner in tow, Clarentine handed me the twitch. A twitch is a simple tool used to neutralize. It's a sturdy, solid wooden pole, about three feet in length, and with a smallish loop secured at one end. This loop is designed to go over the horse's upper lip then to be twisted to tension. Even the strength of a horse could be held firmly in place using the leverage of this pole. I later learned that in most cases this loop is made of nylon rope, but at the end of our twitch was a rusty chain bolted into a circle. The chain gave it that much more biting torque and disincentive against unwanted movement.

Clarentine attached this twitch around Dooner's nose and instructed me to hold it firmly in place and stand a bit to the side. He then pulled out the big buck knife and held it behind his back. He walked toward Dooner using a false, syrupy voice and squatted down nearly under him. I was standing on the far side, so I didn't have a clear view of what he was doing.

Then all at once, this horse made a guttural whimper and lunged forward. At the same time Clarentine stood up, holding the colt's dangling parts at arm's length by his fingertips! There was glee in his face. When I think back on it now, it reminds me of a vicious Viking holding high the cut-off head of his enemy in satisfying triumph.

In stark contrast I gasped in shock from the unexpected butchery of it all. Before I could even catch my next breath, Clarentine tossed the newly cut-off testicles up into the air and, like two large connected turnips, they flew end over end in an arcing trajectory straight into the awaiting jaws of Major, the skinny Doberman who had been standing on the periphery of the action. I wasn't aware that he was there or that he had been eagerly awaiting this very treat. Only one of us had known what was coming.

While the dog enthusiastically chomped down and swallowed his lunch in one large gulp, I reflexively threw up mine. I now see my vomiting in that moment as an authentic response to Clarentine's unchecked cruelty, but back then I only felt shame for what I thought was my weak stomach.

By the time I managed to walk Dooner back to a stall, apologizing to him for what he'd just been made to endure without my knowledge and without anesthesia, I could still hear Clarentine laughing about me being "too sensitive." His teasing was unmerciful, and yet I felt my visceral reaction had betrayed me. In the face of his indoctrination into brutality, showing any form of vulnerability on my part was turning out to be a hazardous liability.

Another heavily etched incident occurred when a large group of townies came to ride horses one lazy Sunday afternoon when I was twelve. It was mostly by word of mouth that people heard about the trail riding we offered. Even first-time riders could come and take out horses by the hour and ride however they wanted in a large open tract of land just across the road. Not many stables rented out trail horses without a guide, so that set us apart.

While this was a welcome means of bringing in extra money for Clarentine, the rest of us complained amongst ourselves about it. These folks usually had no riding experience and were inevitably hard on the mouths and backs of our four-hooved friends.

Clarentine did the calculations and started calling out names: Trusty, Boondocks, Blythe Spirit, Snaggletooth . . . We jumped into action and started tacking up horses to accommodate this large group. "Go grab Little Light." Clarentine directed this command specifically to me. He knew I wouldn't be happy about putting a first-time trail rider on one of my current show ponies, but money was a driving force so I didn't have a say in this decision.

Little Light was a small buckskin pony. Besides being a bold jumper, I loved her gorgeous coloring. Her extremities, head and legs, tail and mane, were a rich black, while the rest of her body was a buttermilk cream color with the distinguishing buckskin black line drawn down the length of her spine. By then I'd shown her a number of times and appreciated her spritely jumping abilities, always clearing the fence by well above the actual height. But she did have a mind of her own and sometimes didn't feel like cooperating. Clarentine regularly denigrated her by claiming that she was as "common as they come." I didn't want Little Light to be exposed to untrained riders, and I didn't think she was going to like it either.

Clenching my jaw and carrying her bridle in hand, I went in search of her in the large paddock. I saw her quietly napping, eyes closed, one hoof cocked in a relaxed way. I hated to have to disturb her but knew I had to strap on the bridle and lead her through the narrow metal gate that separated this particular lot from the tacking area. Other girls were likewise prepping horses for this large group of trail riders. Wrapping the reins around the hitching fence, as was our protocol, I dodged in and out of the awaiting people and went to collect the saddle. That's when it happened. She started to pull.

It began as a firm tug but quickly devolved into a deep straining tension against the constriction of the fence. Perhaps she suddenly realized that she was held in place and hated this fact. I projected that she didn't want a reckless yahoo on her back. Both reasons were understandable. With remarkable vigor she shifted all her weight to her hind legs, baring down as she pulled like dogs do when they have one end of a rope in their teeth and someone holding tight to the other.

As everyone hastily scurried out of the way, all attention turned to this emerging scene. It was a full-force tug-of-war, although Little Light wasn't playing a game. She was determined to break free. It was as if it had become her sole/soul mission. The leather strained and stretched against her weight as she shook her head, bent on being untethered. The scene escalated quickly when Clarentine's voice boomed, "Run git me the twitch!"

I did as he commanded even though every part of me didn't want to obey. Reluctantly I handed him the twitch I'd fetched from the tack room, making me an accessory to what was about to follow.

Grabbing the pole in his rage, he swung it like a mace and caught her smack against her belly. She lurched forward toward the fence, emitting a deep primal groan, then sat back again with a doubled-down strain against the reins that bound her.

"You common bitch! I'm going to break you of this once and for all!" he bellowed as he kept thwacking at her back and buttocks and intermittently upside her head. The whites of her eyes were now showing equal parts fear and rage. She lunged forward to try to get away from the blows that thumped loudly across her rear and sides as he laid down another hit onto her body. Then she jerked back, struggling again against the fence and the confining leather reins with all her might.

Meanwhile Clarentine's face had turned menacingly chiseled, the cords of his neck stood out in demonic strain, and his eyes narrowed to the degree that hers had widened. Having scrambled out of the way, we all were now watching aghast in horrified silence from a short distance. I'd seen his anger before but never to this extent, although as it turns out it would be far from the last time.

Kit and I grabbed each other's hands in a reflexive need for comfort, but there was no escaping the drama we were witnessing. We didn't want to watch and yet were unable to avert our eyes. Hulk against pony, they clashed. She, of sheer will, and he, of abject fury, until suddenly, with one final yank, Little Light tore off the entire top fence board, nails and all, with the leather rein still attached to the newly freed plank. She backed up quickly then turned and trotted off, awkwardly dragging the cumbersome board through the dirt at her hooves.

This dislodged piece of fence seemed to snap Clarentine's vehemence. Like a broken spell, his voice grew measured. He told me to go catch her and put her back in the side field. I found her at the lower barn, her sides heaving and eyes wide.

I spoke softly while moving slowly toward her, hoping to not further spook her. We were both rattled—by what she had just been through and what I had just witnessed. She let me stand beside her so I could separate her knotted bridle from the dragging board. Then I led her to the metal gate that opened to the side field. She trotted out into the grassy area finally unfettered, a small victory for her persistent spirit.

Despite the beating, she had refused to surrender. I remember wondering why she didn't just give in. I was hoping she would so that it would all stop. But would it have? True to her namesake, she had a little light burning brightly inside her. It was who she was, and she wasn't going to let it be extinguished without a fight.

I see in retrospect that my maternal lineage, which taught me to fracture off what otherwise would be emotionally intolerable, kept me from sobbing in horror at the violence I was regularly witnessing. Instead, I created a more palatable narrative that made this somehow acceptable so that I could keep my connection to the horses I loved.

CHAPTER 14

UNWANTED
TRACTION

Meanwhile at a critical threshold in my timeline, the next thing that happened to me threw me into a different kind of crisis. I was thirteen at the time and it was the first day of my summer break. I was riding a new large pony that a man had trailered to the barn that day for training. It was one of those fluky things, like stepping off a curb wrong-footed. It was so routine that I wasn't paying attention. I didn't have a tight enough grip on the reins, so when my new mount tripped, we both did a somersault. My lean girl body and his rotund animal body went head over hooves. The only difference was that after he landed on me, he scrambled back onto his four legs and pranced out of the way, while I lay flattened like a pancake, unable to get up. My thigh seized in sharp pain.

It was when Clarentine ran over, quickly assessed the situation, and announced that he was calling the ambulance that I knew this was bad. When he left to find the telephone, I felt the fear jut up inside me along with the pain of my fractured femur.

It wasn't like I hadn't already been injured before—there was the time I was bucked off and my chin hit a rock, cracking me open like an egg smacked on the side of a mixing bowl. That required stitches and resulted in two bloody towels on the ride to the ER. There were previous bruises, hard falls, and possible concussions because we rarely wore hardhats while riding at the barn, but this was the first time that I actually couldn't get up under my own power. No blood but no mobility either. This seemed worse.

After resetting my leg and drilling a steel rod through the shin bone, they attached a series of weights connected to pulleys and wires. I found myself immobilized on my back in a hospital bed, surrounded by equipment that looked like a contraption drawn partly from a gym and partly from a torture chamber. This would be where I would lie in sharp, intermittent pain for the next two months.

While my friends were showing ponies at the summer shows like Keswick, Farmington, and Roanoke, I was living my days and nights continuously strapped to a hospital bed. After eight weeks of tortuous traction, I thought that I would be released to reset my life and get back on the path of riding again. But I was mistaken. Had this been originally explained to me? Had I just conveniently only heard what I wanted to hear? I'm not sure. Both are possible.

Instead I was discharged wearing a full body cast. I had graduated from hospital confinement to home confinement. Like an Edgar Allan Poe horror story, I was plastered rigidly into a full-length shell that spanned from my toes, around my right leg, clear up to the top of my chest line, which prevented me from bending at the waist. The best I could do was have someone prop me up with pillows like an ironing board on an incline. Not only was I unable to be with the horses and my other friends, but I was now forced to be completely dependent on my mom again, just at the juncture when I was striving for more separation. I appreciate that she took care of me during my convalescence, but at the point that I was desperately trying to differentiate from her, this was the last situation that either of us wanted.

I was reduced to a glorified piñata, a papier-mâché project gone awry. Similarly, I longed to be broken open, to spill out in all directions, to be released from my plastered imprisonment. I hated that cast and longed for the freedom that had been stolen from me.

I also wished to spill out my fears. Would I be able to walk again? Would my leg ever recover? And more importantly, would I be able to ride horses again? But just as the body cast didn't allow me to expose what lay inside that hard shell, my emotional life at home didn't offer room for these conversations either.

I remember the afternoon so fondly when Tess, a riding friend, surprised me by leading Little Elam, one of my favorite ponies, up from the barn to our house. She understood the isolation I was feeling and boldly walked him through the side door halfway into the den where I lay. I hadn't seen any of my horse or pony friends since the accident.

I was thrilled with Elam's unexpected visit to my door. Tess stood beside him in her double pigtails that squirted out from either side above her ears, smiling her sweet smile while leading this haltered gray pony across our brick threshold. There he modestly stood, halfway into our air-conditioned family rec room while his back end remained on the stoop. I could see in my periphery that my mother was fiddling with her collar, a telltale sign that she was just barely containing her disapproval and anxiety about the whole situation.

Encased within my rigid mummy shell, I carefully levered myself upright and crutched my way over to him. I caressed his soft muzzle, patted his thick neck, and twisted my fingers into his coarse, ivory-colored mane. It was like warm molasses drizzled across my insides. I missed him, I missed riding, I missed my life at the barn. The outdoors was vibrantly alive with neighing horses, barking dogs, sunshine, and laughter. Inside this house, inside my cast, I was, in contrast, so rigidly constrained.

Being with Elam ended all too soon, as there was a limit to my ability to stay propped precariously upright on crutches. I resembled Humpty Dumpty ready to fall over at any moment. I also knew there was a cap on this pony's tolerance for having mocha-colored linoleum under his hooves rather than blades of grass. And of course there was a limit to my mother's patience in waiting to regain control of her house.

I watched as pony and friend retreated backward through the doorway to a place I couldn't follow. My elation about this reunion then gave way to grief. The familiar aroma of damp horse hair mixed with a hint of hay and manure musk clung to my hands. Being out of sync with my friends who were engaged in horse shows and their summertime activities made me feel literally like a castaway alone on my deserted island bed.

When I finally rehabbed my way back to the barn later that fall, I was chomping at the bit to pick up the reins and get back in the saddle again. And I was certainly ready to be out of house quarantine. I later wondered if this accident and having to be unnaturally tied to home during that pivotal teenage summer propelled me with even more urgency into a life at the stables than I might have felt otherwise. This ordeal ricocheted me back to the barn with a greater determination to reclaim my independent life and sense of belonging there. My strong desire to individuate from my parents, however, resulted in making me that much more dependent on Clarentine. The cost of inverting the importance of these relationships was lost on me back then.

I was thrilled to finally be back to riding again that October, but circumstances had changed while I was away. For one thing, I had grown during my absence. My legs now draped disproportionately down my ponies' sides. I tried to compensate by shortening my stirrups and tucking my knees, but I had to face the fact that I would never be the right build to remain a jockey. It was visibly clear that I was too tall to show ponies any longer.

Although Clarentine had been discussing my graduation to horses, it was still a surprise when he announced, "I'm putting you on Critter this weekend." This would mean jumping larger fences—by at least a foot—as well as competing against adults. But the prospect of entering the arena on a horse brought new possibilities, and I relished the opportunity.

I assume that onlookers saw me ride over a standard round of jumps that day on my matte chestnut-colored horse, but for me it signaled a new era. Not only was I back in the saddle now riding horses on the weekly show riding circuit, but I would also be competing for higher stakes. The new exhilarations of this came with increased pressure from Clarentine to win.

CHAPTER 15

THE BREAKING

W ithin this context of constant exposure to and justification of the brutality at the barn, I took another step in the perpetuation of violence when I began helping Clarentine with the breaking of new horses. It would be decades before the idea of horse whispering came into mainstream equine consciousness. But even so it would never have been welcomed at his stables.

Clarentine's goals were always and only accomplished through subjugation. I remember the first time he directed me to "break" a horse using this same mentality. The young colt in question had been dropped off a few days before. Clarentine had begun his training by strapping a heavy Western saddle onto his unaccustomed back and leaving it in place for a number of days. Now, of course, the cruelty of giving no break from the rubbing of the saddle against delicate backs and withers and the tightness of the girth around young bellies is obvious, but back then it was Clarentine's practice of what worked. That became the only necessary justification.

He led this brown colt into the ring and shut the gate behind. Then he called to me to approach cautiously. I ran my open hand down his neck and spoke softly to him. Clarentine held the reins as well as a lunge line that was clipped to his bridle and launched me up into the air. As quietly as possible I threw my right leg over the colt's narrow body, landing softly into the saddle strapped to his back. Adding my body weight was a new variable to the equation. One never could be sure how a young horse would respond to this experience.

I could feel his skittish energy under me, a muscular package of trembling nerves. These were incredibly tense moments because how a young horse would act in this new situation was completely unpredictable. They might rear up on their hindquarters and/or catapult forward in a bucking series on their front legs. They might dart sharply to one side or another or take off in a bolting gallop. Or they might decide that it's acceptable and be okay without a fuss. Horses have a customized response all their own as any bronco rider will attest. However, in the rodeo circumstances, much is already known about the trademark moves of each particular horse that the cowboys lottery to ride. In contrast, this would be a new experience for us all, the horse too.

My heart rate pulsed from the tension of not knowing what was going to happen next. The seconds ticked by as I felt the tension build below my seat.

"Click to him," Clarentine commanded me to urge him forward.

In addition to making these sounds, I added pressure from my inner legs against his sides. Nothing happened. Again, I clicked and squeezed.

"Kick 'em."

I followed with more insistent kicks of my heels and more clicks from my mouth, but he refused to move.

Clarentine then walked up to me slowly so as not to alert the colt to his plan and handed me a crop that he had been concealing behind his back. This crop was a short, stiff stick with an extra flap of leather sewn on one end to apply a stinging effect.

He stood back and said, "Give him the signal, then let him have it." I urged him forward again, hoping I wouldn't need to use it. Still he didn't move. I sparingly tapped the crop across his hind end. He remained quivering in place.

"Harder!" Clarentine bellowed. I complied with what I considered to be my version of harder, and still the colt dug in where he stood.

"Ya better make him do right or I'll jerk ya off right now and git me a rider that can!" he threatened.

So I obliged. Saying "no" was never an option. I gave the colt a stronger thwack that carried meaning and heard the accompanied sound of the leather stick resound across hindquarters from my own blow. He lunged-lurched forward to another standstill. At Clarentine's insistence, I put more behind this, starting from a higher arc above my head for added momentum. Round after round I continued with this repeated *thwack, thwack!* The colt leapt to get away from each hit, then jerked to a stop. I was instructed to keep at it, my arm growing weary with the repetitive lashes.

Finally, Clarentine called it a day and released us both. The colt was damp with nervous sweat. We had both been trained that day. The colt had a lesson in being wary of humans, while I splintered off another part of myself—the part connected to my humanity.

CHAPTER 16

OUR RELATIONSHIP WITH AUTHORITY

I t would be many years yet before I would first hear about Milgram's Shock Experiment, but I remember it well. It was the fall semester of my freshman year in college, and I was running late that morning for my introductory psychology class. Scurrying across the extensive limestone campus, I recall taking a seat in the large hall along with the other straggling students who were similarly shaking off sleep.

The professor that autumn day somberly prefaced his talk by noting that the experiment he was about to discuss was so unethical that it could never again be replicated. And yet, he added with emphasis, "... to overlook the results will be at our own peril." Then he began describing Milgram's experiment, a controversial study conducted in the basement of a building on Yale's campus in 1963. The experiment was initially described to the participants as a study related to memory. The real agenda was much more nefarious. It was designed to observe the internal conflict between obeying authority on the one hand and honoring one's moral values on the other.

Each unsuspecting participant was individually brought into the room and instructed to start giving a memory test to the student (unbeknownst to them, a paid actor). The volunteer was directed to correct any mistakes by administering a small jolt of electricity. For each additional wrong answer, the voltage of the shock was to be increased. They were told this disincentive method was being studied as a means to increase recall functioning.

The levels of electrical voltage were labeled *Slight Shock* all the way up to *Danger: Severe Shock* and were visually displayed on the machine dashboard in front of them. As the experiment went on, each volunteer was encouraged by the lab assistant to continue to increase the intensity of the shocks given to their peer with every subsequent error. The grunts and groans from this student could be heard through the intercom system with each increase.

Whenever a volunteer wondered out loud if maybe they should stop, the lab assistant insisted they keep going with the experiment using statements like, "It is absolutely essential that you continue," and "You have no other choice; you must go on." Meanwhile Milgram and his team were observing how long these volunteers would override their own ethical values by deferring to the presumed authority in the room, in this case, the lab assistant.

The results were startling. The participants as a whole continued to shock their fellow human being for much longer than hypothesized. In one extreme case, despite the volunteer believing that his fellow participant had a bad heart and that administering more shocks might kill him, he continued to deliver higher and higher levels of electric shocks without an apparent end in sight.

While the general degree of compliance with authority varied, this study starkly demonstrated that we are primed to obey those in authority even at the expense of our own moral conscience. Unfortunately, both history and our current world affairs are rife with horrific examples confirming this.

I was riveted and disturbed while listening to my professor relate these alarming outcomes back in that college lecture hall that day, but at the same time, I was also unconsciously segmenting off the full force of the uncomfortable comparison between my obedience to Clarentine and the similarity with these participants. He held all the power at the apex of his hierarchy. Through the leverage he wielded, he had no trouble recruiting me and others to do his bidding. For our part, we had been conditioned to obey authority while locking away any moral distress that it caused us.

When debriefing the participants of this experiment afterward, it was also difficult for these volunteers to assimilate the full implications of this experiment and their own complicity in the violence of it. They got foggy or justified their aggressive actions as just following orders. The psychological term for this is *cognitive dissonance*.

It's so difficult to tolerate the discrepancy that exists between how we see ourselves and our actual behavior. We become attached to the self-image we project into the world. So much so that whatever doesn't fit with the ways that we want to see ourselves, we outright dismiss in our minds and thus omit from our narratives. Like a powerful sedative, no one wants to see their capacity for aggression. These revisionist stories we tell ourselves then serve to justify any discordant actions in order to keep our ego intact.

There's no denying that, back then, I not only obeyed but also rationalized my actions. I kept this story intact for many years. We can't dismantle conditioning that we don't recognize or don't allow ourselves to see. It is another function of our stories—to obscure difficult truths.

As I began to work through the additional stratum of my past in therapy, I had to face the reality that I was somewhere along this same spectrum as Milgram's research subjects. I was willing to abdicate my moral compass by being obedient to a man who led through domination, fear, and abuse. When we aren't able to repair these splits, we learn to discard our humanity instead. I had become complicit with the toxic environment of the stables. When I did open my eyes to this later on, it was a terrifying realization.

How I justified my participation in the violence at the barn came not only from what I inhaled there or absorbed through my personal family legacy. My narrative was also fortified by our culture's status quo, which has historically rationalized inhumane acts toward those being "othered." I began to see that whenever a structure is built on notions of "better than," it requires oppression to keep power concentrated at the top. In this way, subjugating others serves an intended purpose. When this form of suppression permeates into our very pores, it is hard to recognize what has been absorbed and the impact it is continuing to have on our thoughts and behaviors in the world. But the fact remains that all of us who hold privilege in such a system are in collusion with this perpetuated violence.

As Gary guided me on the archaeological dig into what happened to me in those developmentally fundamental years, I began to excavate other ways that aggression and my rationalizations about it were operating inside me and how all this was tied to the current crisis in my marriage.

CHAPTER 17

MY MIRRORED
REFLECTION

Our greatest desire is to be seen and accepted for who we are. Our greatest fear is that we will be rejected if fully known. I struggled to not judge myself harshly for the ways that I was beginning to see new layers of my aggression in action. I feared the worst when this shadow work was out in the open. However, to my surprise, Gary met me not with rejection but with kindness.

"We are all in the PR business. No one wants to recognize the hurt we are capable of inflicting on others. No one likes to see their ugly self," he began. "It doesn't line up with the image we hold so dear. It doesn't fit with the way we strive to market our ego to others."

Our compulsion to hide behind a hologram projection of ourselves gets developed early on for a host of reasons: traumatic events and our inaccurate interpretations, to be sure, but also children's tendency to personalize, ancestral inheritances, and our own proclivities can all contribute to not feeling we are enough just as we are. The fact that we are all innately worthy somehow gets dislodged. Then from these negative stories that we unwittingly carry about ourselves, we feel a need to boost our self-inventory scores and cultivate a persona that we come to believe is the real us. It is our unconscious and creative attempt at emotional self-survival. However, it is this very distortion that later causes harm to us and others.

"Look, the fact is everyone is aggressive," Gary zoomed out. "Everyone has harmed, impacted, or caused pain to others." He went on to explain that besides the most obvious kinds of aggression, there is also control, manipulation, omission, placation, superiority, inferiority, and even misplaced caretaking. Basically, whenever we mess with the sovereign rights of others, we are being harmful. We all have resistance to seeing the violence we well-meaning people perpetuate, but it's not a matter of intention—it is about the impact our actions have. This is part of our human fallibility. But it only makes it worse when we continue to try to hide or deny this from ourselves and others. Gary's boiled-down philosophy was that if we can just get our ego out of the way enough to see our aggression, then we have a fighting chance of taking responsibility for it and, importantly, of not acting from it.

Before Mark had put our relationship on the line, I still wore blinders, obscuring my own capacity to cause harm. I took him for granted, dismissed his needs, wanted him to go along with what was most convenient—what was comfortable for me. And I wasn't particularly open to his feedback about any of this. If the marriage dynamic is built on an underlying power struggle of who's right and who's wrong, then everything can become a battlefield. How activities get scheduled, how we drive or how we are passengers in the car, how the dishwasher is loaded . . . The paper cuts inflicted by origami swords can be endless.

"How could I be so awful?" I began to crumble into shame halfway through this therapy session. Gary reminded me that viewing ourselves as we are, not just the image of who we think we are, actually gives us a starting point for this work. However, not missing a beat, he also cautioned to watch out for the tendency we all have to collapse, either into self-judgment or projected blame. When we operate out of the delusion that we aren't enough, there is little room for just being curious self-explorers.

Coming to accept the fact that we are all aggressive is a process that my own clients have come to affectionately describe as "eating the death cookie." It feels like annihilation and in a way, it is, but it is just our egos that are being asked to surrender command central. Who we have come to believe we are is only our outward-facing personality constructed as a result of what has happened to us, fueled by the stories we tell ourselves and the fears festering within us.

"Relationships are the hardest thing we ever attempt to do," Gary continued. "All that we haven't worked through from our past gets amplified and expressed with our intimate partners. However . . ." Gary continued, ". . . because relationships can bring out the worst in us, they also hold the greatest possibility for our growth."

Gary would throw out these incredible nuggets. I couldn't always appreciate the fullness of their truth in the moment, but this one was like a warm breeze. If I hoped to deepen my connection with Mark, bringing awareness to the ways that I am aggressive would be my first radical act of love.

CHAPTER 18

THE DRIVE

B ack at the barn, my childhood exposure to physical and sexual violence continued to escalate. The temperature of the abuse had been heating up so slowly that I could hardly register it. I was fourteen at the time and my newest barn buddy, Kelly, and I were dividing up sections of hay bales to feed to the horses at the lower barn when Clarentine called out to me.

"C'mon, jump in. We're goin' for a ride," he asserted while pointing toward the van.

My stomach pitched. I wanted to get some lunch and a cold drink if we were going to the Ivy Store, but I didn't want to go on a longer excursion. The prospect of being in the truck alone with him now set my insides on alert, but I was also conditioned to appreciate the attention. At that time, he hadn't pressed me further than what had become a steady intake of dirty jokes, innuendos, flirting comments, and constant leering. We were all unnaturally accustomed to this, but I innocently still thought that I was somehow immune from him pressing this further.

Regardless, he hadn't asked a question. It was an order. So I trailed after him and obediently opened the passenger side door to the van to hoist myself up the steep step to get inside.

The bench seat was a hard, dark vinyl surface that sported random slashes exposing the underbelly cotton-white material. I sat close to the door, leaving the large open space between us. Clarentine jammed the long, thin gear shift bar into position through some muscled wrestling with an expletive thrown in for added measure. The van reminded me of a recalcitrant elephant. Lumbering and cumbersome in body, always reluctant to move forward and even more so when asked to go in reverse.

I saw Kelly watching us as we headed down the long driveway. It felt special to be picked to ride solo with him, and yet . . . I was aware on some level that it marked me at the same time. When he left with other riders, I would secretly note it, wonder what it meant, and consider the outcome. He used favoritism to cultivate this distance and competitiveness between us. The dangling threat of being taken off a horse and having to watch someone else get to ride instead was ever-present. This was the power he flaunted. I imagined that the girls back at the barn would now be wondering where we were going and guessing what we might be doing. Worrying about what the others might be thinking weighed on me as I rolled down the bumpy road alone in the truck with him.

When we turned out of West Leigh and zoomed past the Ivy Store, I knew with a rock in my gut that this would be a longer outing. I was strong for my age, so he would sometimes take me to get loads of hay. I would stack bales in the back of the truck as he threw them in from the fields. But I could tell that this wasn't on today's agenda either. The fact is, I didn't know where we were headed or for how long we would be gone. I started calculating the time and hoped that I would make it back before my absence at dinner at home would be noticed.

Oblivious to my discomfort, or perhaps not, Clarentine was chatting up a storm, talking about the new horse that was recently dropped off for training. "That one's got good bones and a long stride," he assessed out loud. "Might buy him if it turns out he got anything between his ears." On the outside, I nodded with agreement and laughed on cue at the right moments of his story, yet on the inside, I was strung tight. I liked the special focus until I didn't.

He punctuated his last clever comment with a swig from the Coke bottle he held lodged between his legs. He was never far from a gulp of his favorite bourbon and Coke drink, as I was quite familiar with, and drinking it while driving a vehicle out on the road was no exception. We continued heading west toward the Blue Ridge Mountains that played peek-a-boo with us around particular curves in the road. With each mile I ventured a guess as to what might be his destination—and intent. The grain store, which would take us all the way to Crozet? Some unknown family farm to look at a horse? Somewhere else? He hadn't said.

I was somewhat relieved when we pulled into the liquor store. Virginia was governed by Blue Laws back then, and these Alcoholic Beverages Control (or ABC) stores were state-run and provided the only means of buying liquor. Because the stores were monopolies, no cost was wasted on appearances. They were brown, stand-alone, windowless, uniform square buildings that reminded me of pictures I'd seen of the Alamo. Their hours and days were strictly controlled, so there was often a rush to get there before closing time and prior to dry Sundays.

"Be right back," he said as he put the truck into park and hopped out of the cab. I watched from my front seat perch as he and his cowboy boots strolled confidently through the narrow front door of the store. A short time later, he emerged carrying a brown-bagged bottle. I didn't have to see what was inside to know what it contained. In the other hand he held a bottle of Coke.

As I'd now witnessed countless times before, he poured out a generous amount of the dark soda and added the familiar Old Crow bourbon. Then with his fat thumb held over the top, he swirled the copper liquid into the dark-colored cola. Then he raised the bottle to his lips and took a long chug.

"Here, have a swig," he said as he handed me the blended drink.

"No, thanks," I casually countered.

"Ah, c'mon, just a nip won't kill ya." I mostly didn't want to put my mouth where his had been since I had watched the wetness of his saliva cover the thin opening of the bottle. I cringed at the thought of his back swill too. Always overriding these innate apprehensions, I took it anyway. Timidly tipping the contoured glass toward my own lips, I feigned a quick sip.

"Ya can do better than that." So I complied and turned the bottle upward, gulping down one noteworthy swallow. Although it wasn't my first time, it still came as a surprise at how the alcohol entered my mouth at first stealthy and smooth, then scratching the back of the throat with a searing heat clear down to my gullet. How could something taste both like liquid amber butter and yet sharp like ripened jalapenos? It was similar to a warm whinny followed by an unexpected mule kick.

"That's more like it," he reinforced.

To my relief, he started up the van and, from the parking lot, turned our vehicle in the direction back toward the barn. Before then I wasn't sure if this was the destination or just a pit stop on the way to somewhere else. I felt a current of relief that didn't last long.

After a few moments of silence and using the seductive voice I had come to recognize, he crooned, "Come over here a little closer. You're so far away."

"Nah, I'm good over here," I said, trying to pretend a casual response in contradiction to my tightening innards. He reacted by reaching out with his free hand and gripping my forearm with a pressure that scared me. Having hold of me, he pulled me next to him by sliding my whole body involuntarily across the slippery vinyl surface.

"Now, that's better," he stated, pleased with the new configuration.

I pushed off his hefty torso in order to slide myself back over and reclaim my space near the window with a feigned laugh. I was aware by then of the precarious balance between cajoling and flattering him while also not giving him the wrong idea—or pissing him off. The term *fawning* has only recently been added to the fight/flight/freeze defense responses for when our nervous systems become overwrought. I didn't have the word for this back then, but trying to appease Clarentine in this way became an unconscious strategy for me.

At the same time that I was now trying to pacify his advances, I also grabbed the large metal handle on the door next to me. This old-style, unwieldy shaft was used to laboriously roll the window up or down. Now I wondered if I could crank it open in a hurry if I needed to yell for help. Would it be quicker to open the door and jump out? But I knew these weren't viable options as we were barreling down this rural stretch of road. Instead, I just held tightly to the metal handle like it was a lifeline.

"You're supposed to be driving," I managed to squeak out.

"I'm drivin' just fine," he retorted, displaying a new tightness in his jaw.

There was no getting out of this. It was just he and I, and I had seen what happened to the horses that put up resistance. I'd also seen him turn on people, cast them out of his life with harsh retribution. There could be hell to pay for disobeying and being on his bad side.

While he stared at the road, I felt the deflating effect of his withdrawal of attention. It's as if the sun had just been obliterated by a front of menacing clouds. We drove the awkward rest of the way back to the stables in strained silence.

CHAPTER 19

EXODUS FROM THE BARN

A few weeks later, Kit didn't show up at the barn. She was absent the next day and the following. Her exodus was as simple and unrippled as that. When I called her, she said she was busy being a barn hand at a different stable. By then, she and I weren't in the same school and our friendship had grown more distant, so although I would run into her occasionally, our paths quietly diverged.

It was around that same time that the mother of another rider at the barn called after dinner one evening asking to talk to my mom. I didn't find out about what was discussed until the next day when my mom stopped me in the kitchen as I was grabbing a snack before heading to the barn.

Almost like an accusation against me, she tartly began, "Mrs. Miller called to talk about Clarentine last night."

"What about him?" I asked with a reactive sharpness in my own voice. I was already reflexively habituated to defend and protect him. I was also reading her irritation about having to be bothered by this as if it were my fault.

I gather the conversation with this mom started off something to the effect of, "Do you know what is happening down at the barn? Have you noticed what is going on?" Turns out she made this same call to a number of the other moms telling each of them that she was taking her daughter away from the stables and encouraging them to do the same. Over the years, some parents had just quietly extracted their daughters from the scene without a backward glance. This mom was one of the few ever willing to overtly raise the warning flag.

I don't recall the exact euphemism my mom used in that conversation with me. Some phrase akin to "I hear that he likes girls" or "has a thing for his young riders." What I do remember is that she didn't specifically ask if any of this was happening to me. That would have been much too direct.

Pausing awkwardly, my mom asked if this was true.

It was a pivotal moment. I was already uncomfortable with the way that he ogled my body, told dirty jokes, and winked and leered in my direction. Then there was the recent incident in the truck. But under what circumstances would I have jeopardized my connection with these horses I loved? Certainly not the one I was in. Besides, I still believed I was handling all this just fine.

I took a breath and said that it wasn't true, that it was an exaggeration, that there was nothing to worry about. In short, I lied and dismissed this other mom's concern for all of us. But at the time, I had also been armoring myself to believe that it wasn't so bad. I had become so adept at contorting to this version of truth that I had convinced myself there was nothing to worry about. I was laying the groundwork for my Faustian bargain.

"Well, all right," she announced in a voice softened with relief. It was the answer she wanted to believe, the reassurance she wanted to hear. She was more than ready to put all of this aside and start prepping for dinner. I was likewise relieved that this talk was over so quickly and I could now go to the barn.

To be able to see abuse, you have to be willing to be uncomfortable. To acknowledge it means that there would be a responsibility to intervene. It becomes much easier to shut one's eyes. Neither one of us wanted things to change. The arrangement served us both.

CHAPTER 20

PATERNAL LINEAGE

"Where was your dad in all this? Why do you keep protecting him?" Gary, as usual, deep-dove into the conversation without preamble. My parents had adopted the traditional gender roles of their respective legacies and their era. That arrangement meant my mother reigned over all things domestic, including parenting. My father was fine with relegating all things daughter and horse to my mother. Why would he intervene? This was out of his assigned territory, and although the boundaries were only implied, this demarcation was clearly mutually benefi-cial. Their marital bargain mostly kept things humming along, seemingly conflict-free.

I did bristle when my mother was critical of him and some-times stood up for him when she lashed out callously. I admired my dad as the steady, patient, generous one. In my narrative, he got to be the good parent. I viewed their arguments as if he had no agency to change how she treated him. There is a tendency in all of us to evaluate things in polarizing terms—good/bad, right/wrong, either/or. The both/and muscles don't get in enough reps.

"Keep in mind that your father is getting something out of their arrangement too. He isn't a victim of his own marriage," reflected Gary. "It serves him to have your mom be the ogre in the family. Then he gets to look like the saint. Besides, his own comfort was kept intact by avoiding conflict with her. He prioritized this over addressing the issues between them."

It was always harder for me to see my dad's complicit part in the bargain he and my mother had forged together. There's a reason behind casting one parent in the hero role. I wanted to believe that I had at least one parent in my camp. The alternative is akin to being emotionally orphaned. However, I could see how his unwillingness to challenge my mother also meant that her unrestrained anxiety hailed down on me and my brother instead. Additionally, with my mother cast in this role, my father never had to look at the ways his privileged position in the family went unexamined and resulted in undermining her own.

As we started to dig deeper into the inquiry Gary had opened, I began to wonder about the ancestral legacy behind why my father deferred his parenting role. Even beyond the generational norms of his time, this abdication seemed somehow more disconnected and extreme. A story about my grandfather's trauma started to take on a more resonant meaning for my own life as I began to see how this lineage shaped my father and also contributed to setting me up for the unmonitored grooming and abuse that happened at the barn.

My dad's father—my grandfather—was an only child, born into a family of considerable means in 1898. Alongside the obvious benefits of privilege was a gentrified culture that regularly outsourced their offspring. "Children should be seen but not heard" was the parenting motto of the time. Having been raised by full-time governesses, at ten years old, young Billy was shipped off to boarding school during the academic year and on to various summer camps during the time between semesters. When he turned thirteen, his parents sent him to a working horse ranch in New Mexico for the entire summer. Although this was an unusual option at the time, there was a distant connection with the ranch owner, and it was a place where he could be off-loaded until school started again. Child-rearing for the elite was always optional—and well-resourced.

I wonder what my grandfather was thinking and feeling as he boarded a train, leaving the soot gray industrial area of Chicago bound for distant lands, alone, far from everyone and everything he knew. Was he wondering why he was being shuffled away again? Or had he already acclimated to the expectations of independence and stoicism for boys on their way to becoming men in their culture of that day? Undoubtedly, feelings were already considered a handicap in any circumstance, so I imagine he bit back any creeping tendrils of fear and "manned up."

Arriving at a remote station amid the earth-baked hues of the spacious Southwest must have felt otherworldly—and it was. On the working ranch he would learn how to ride horses (boys too can feel hoofbeats in their blood), herd cattle, and sleep in bunkhouses shared with ranch hands—all of which he later mused offered more of an "education" than his prep school ever did. The muscle-building work, the feel of leather, and the wide open vistas were all a far cry from his life of books and fancy finger bowls.

However, the comfort of that world was about to be set atilt. After laboriously carving the country on the steel snake of a train ride back home at the end of the summer, there was no one at the train station to greet him! I imagine the disappointment must have shown in his posture as he waited and waited, then bent to pick up his leather-worn duffel bag, still dusty from the trail, and walked the last few miles to his house on the outskirts of Chicago.

Finally arriving outside his front door, he turned the handle, only to discover that the door was uncharacteristically locked. So he knocked. Surprisingly, the man who answered wasn't his father. Through the mutually wary conversation that followed, he was told in some fashion, "No, your parents aren't here . . . In fact, they don't live here anymore . . . We moved into this house this summer . . . No, they didn't leave a forwarding address." While still taking in this situation, the man concluded, "Can you please leave now?" and punctuated his goodbye with the close of the door. My thirteen-year-old grandfather was left standing dumbfounded on the doorstep of his house, which was now occupied by complete strangers.

How could his parents have moved without telling him?

It's true that this era predated the invention of telephones, but there were telegrams and train schedules. Also information could have been left with the family who had purchased the house. I try to imagine this scene and the heft of it on the boy who would become my grandfather. Kids can't help but feel implicated by what happens to them. With all that he'd already experienced, this moment must have further reinforced his concerns about not belonging, not measuring up, not being worthy of consideration. Why else would they send him away at every opportunity?

He did eventually locate his parents. Turns out they had moved into the city to a fashionable apartment because it was more conveniently located. My grandfather, when he told me this story—more than once—never mentioned any acknowledgment of remorse or guilt from his parents about what this experience of abandonment had felt like for him. Like most children, learning to swallow the actions and justifications of loved ones becomes adaptive. It helps to silence the inconvenient feelings that might otherwise bubble up. So instead, like a bird thrown early out of the nest, he learned to fend for himself and accept this expectation of "manhood" with an air of loneliness and quiet resignation that continued to hover around him all his life. These are the familial and cultural messages and modeling that then got paid forward through what my dad learned about parenting.

CHAPTER 21

THREE KINDS
OF FAMILIES

"My parents did the best they could," I said, feeling a sudden urge to defend them in my next therapy session. I could criticize my parents, but it was harder to hear this from others. Besides, I still wanted to think of them as having been good parents. Toggling back and forth between loyalty and anger is hilly terrain.

What Gary said next has stuck with me ever since.

"There are three kinds of families," he began. "The good, the bad, and the real. You may have had a 'good' family, but it doesn't sound like you had a 'real' one."

This distinction immediately fish-hooked my attention.

My family, like all families, have their hardships and pains, losses and traumas. But what distinguishes a real family is how these events and feelings are addressed. It is true that sometimes my home felt like an oasis, but at other times, it was an emotionally arid desert. When I think back, I can see how we never directly addressed emotional issues. We couldn't seem to resolve conflict through a sustained conversation. Our nuclear system became quickly overwhelmed by feelings to the point that boxes full of painful memories collected dust in our attic for decades, and unresolved issues continued to cast long, unspoken shadows.

The Danish are a stoic people who are also as soft as their famous pastries. I wish I had been privy to my mom's gooey insides. That would have offered me a real connection and given me permission to explore my own inner stickiness. Instead, my mother kept these parts to herself, and I got her leftover crusty bits.

I was met with her caricature. She looked the part and said the right things at times, but at the first hint of emotionally uneven ground, she would collapse—either by running from the room or by becoming viciously angry, then running from the room.

My adaptation to minimize conflict and tiptoe around prickly issues was consistently reinforced. Learning to scrap my emotions, my sense of self, and any validation for my experiences was often an easier route. The appearance of family harmony at the expense of real connection was promoted as a sign of a "good" family.

My father's English heritage was Victorian-rooted. Words like "proper" and "gentlemanly" conveyed what was valued along with the reserved stance it required. My dad marched to this prescribed drumbeat of the culture where men's emotions were considered a handicap and women's were to be placated. That meant his internal life was as constricted as my mom's.

The familial form of conditioning I experienced was not intentionally malicious—far from it—it's just that my parents, as all parents, were subject to the forces that had shaped them, along with the propensity to unconsciously play out these influences in succession down the generational line. My family on both sides came from a long line of adept contortionists in the face of pain and trauma.

In the real family that Gary was referencing, there is a mutual willingness to enter into emotionally difficult conversations. There is implicit respect for the distinct experiences of every member. The atmosphere is one where mistakes and hurts can be acknowledged and validated. There is support for everyone's learning and growth. The discomfort that comes with change is embraced and navigated together. And feelings don't run the risk of being evaluated as bad or unacceptable.

This is the family modeling that most of us didn't get, especially in our hierarchically based culture where perfectionism is exalted as a goal and the humanness of making mistakes is seen as a failure. We live in a society where, in general, appearances are valued over vulnerability, where defending replaces validating, where differences are perceived as a threat, and where aggression of all kinds is justified as an unspoken means of maintaining the status quo.

Within this context, it is also seductive for a "good" family to cast aspersions onto a "bad" family. This judgment avoids looking at what is emotionally missing from both kinds of home environments and the cost it extracts from everyone.

According to this astute definition, real families are indeed a rarity.

CHAPTER 22

FARGO

Rallying against the constriction of appearances in the ways that I could at fifteen, I became disillusioned with competing in the hunter jumper divisions. In these classes, every round was evaluated based on the consistency of each jumped fence and the equitation of horse and rider throughout the round. Here the subjective preferences of each judge played such a large role. Biased opinions and the possibility of having personal favorites seemed like it might too easily influence the outcome. After all, I was well aware that I rode for someone who could and did generate his own controversy wherever he went.

In contrast, how horse and rider looked while jumping didn't matter when it came to competing in open stadium jumping divisions. One's performance was based purely on the number of cleared fences and the time it took to complete a round. If a horse and rider pulled a pole, went off course, refused a fence, or exceeded the time limits, it was clear-cut: they wouldn't qualify for the next round. The performance was either objectively clean or it wasn't. This objective sense of fairness appealed to me.

Therefore, when Clarentine signed me up for my first open jumping class I was excited—and terrified. It meant that the fences would not only be bigger from the start but would also be generously raised throughout the class. However, my love of jumping outweighed the trepidation I simultaneously felt.

My mother tried to dissuade me from entering into this type of competition. Just the thought of it frightened her. She had long ago stopped coming to even the occasional show. It was hard enough for her to watch me jump over regular-sized pony fences, let alone now the prospect of much larger obstacles. On one level I could understand why. It was dangerous, but I had a gusto for the challenge, and her keeping a distance from my world suited me fine. I embraced the independence of having my own life with horses that didn't include her.

For others, watching horse and rider hurdle over complex jump courses was always a crowd pleaser. The inherent excitement and risks drew in the spectators. Audiences were good for revenue, and in order to entice entries, the cash prizes grew in proportion to the height of the fences. For Clarentine, open jumping was a means of generating more winnings. This was where the money was.

He decided the horse and rider pairings, and when he assigned me to Fargo, we quickly became a dynamic jumping duo. Fargo was a mixed breed, part Thoroughbred, part quarter horse Appaloosa. He had a deep sable-colored coat, a thick neck, and a stocky build with a blanket across his hindquarters, a white-quilted area embellished with brown and black spots covering his rump. So while he had some of the features of a Thoroughbred from the girth forward, this rear end area gave away his Appaloosa heritage. Although not an obvious combination to produce a jumper of his caliber, he had the disposition and passion for flying through the air that far exceeded his motley bloodline.

At 15.2 hands, he was considered a small horse, but he made up for it with a big heart and a mountain of courage. He willingly launched us both over any fence put in front of him, even the jumps that were taller than he could see over. He never refused a fence, and Clarentine always marveled that he was like a cat on his feet—able to get out of trouble by managing to stay upright on all fours. I always felt safe on his back when we were hurtling through space.

In addition to his less-than-pedigreed looks, Fargo pranced at fences with a bouncy gait full of paprika and cayenne rather than the steady canter of a champion hunter. He was staccato, not legato. However, the goal in the open jumping divisions was only to get over the fence clean, without faults. The "how" was not important. This was where the real action would be, and Fargo and I wanted a go at it.

On a personal level, jumping bigger, taller fences gave me an even stronger sensation of flying through the air. And Fargo loved to jump as much as I did. Even on lazy afternoons at the stables when he was congregating with his equine friends in the fields casually swishing flies off each other's faces, Fargo, for no apparent reason, would get a burr up his bum. As the designated leader, he would suddenly ignite his quietly relaxing companions into a synchronized, all-out gallop around the field that would grow more and more frenzied. The herd of them running in coordinated stride one beside another, but willy-nilly in their zigzagged path, reminded me of my own pack of teenage friends driving hand-me-down clunker cars on country roads in a similarly reckless fashion.

Back in the field, Fargo would then, at some fever pitch moment, break away from the rest of the group and solo jump the five-foot railed fence of the large enclosure. Each time I witnessed this, I would smile with conspiratorial delight and wonder what motivated him. Just the pure joy of it? Because he knew he could? To show off for the mares? To get that elusive blade of grass on the other side? I didn't know back then why I did the things I did, and I imagine Fargo didn't either. We were both just spirited and independent like that. That's what made us a well-matched team.

But at the time of that first show, I didn't know any of this, as we hadn't molded a relationship, and I was a tense bundle of nerves. It would be my first competition over fences starting at four and a half feet rather than the three-foot, six-inch hunter height. The jumps would be raised with each round. And I would be riding against adults, some of them professionals.

The course consisted of a wide variety of fences, like what one can now watch on TV. It included colorfully designed brick and stone walls, gates and poles, fancy coops, brushes, and combinations. The goal was to make the course challenging enough to weed out a percentage of riders on each round but not so difficult as to eliminate everyone.

The only schooling fences we had at our stables were made out of rusted barrels and standards set in customized truck tires. Naturally worn wooden poles sat on plain iron pegs. No fences had wings. Nothing was painted. Our brush fence was made out of temporary evergreen branches hastily cut and piled up in front.

In other words, none of the fences we practiced jumping over looked anything like these that I was now staring at. Like the difference between watching a familiar black-and-white film and suddenly sitting in a colorful IMAX movie, I wondered if Fargo was experiencing any of the same intimidating awe I was feeling in this moment.

My mind started to go blank. My voice sounded squeaky to my own ears. I felt a droplet of sweat roll down the inside of my shirt. Would I be able to incorporate all this information when I was feeling so much anxiety? I wasn't at all sure.

The order of ride was always decided lottery style and posted prior to the class. I silently prayed that I wouldn't have to go first. I also didn't want to go last. There seemed to me a special pressure inherent in either one of these polar positions. Either I would have to be the first to blaze the trail or I would have to wait and watch too many other riders take their turns, which would give my nerves too much time to wreak havoc on my stomach.

The order was decided, and I would be riding first.

Now adding to my worries, I feared that I wouldn't be able to remember the twists and turns of the course. It was always one thing to see the diagram of the course thumb-tacked up on the board and quite another thing entirely to ride a horse over each jump in the proper order with onlooking spectators. The course would also be altered and made more challenging with each subsequent round.

Long after I gave up riding, the residue of this anxiety would regularly visit me at night. Rather than flashes of being unprepared for an exam or not being able to find a classroom,

I instead would dream of having forgotten some difficult jump course.

As Fargo and I waited on deck just outside the gate for the class to start, I tried to soothe my galloping nerves. I would discover that these anticipatory times were always the most excruciating. In what would become a regular practice, I leaned over to stroke Fargo's neck and whisper in his ear, "We can do this." I was not at all convinced, but by reassuring him, I was of course attempting to reassure myself. It was in this moment that Clarentine came up beside us and handed me his plastic cup.

"Here, have a sip of this," he encouraged. By this point I was familiar with this drink and in that moment welcomed the warm, burning sensation that poured some liquid courage into my body.

"Now ride him right," he succinctly commanded.

Our number was called and Fargo and I trotted into the ring. While completing the standard warm-up circle, I was acutely aware that the stands were full and the ring was lined with eager fans. A blanketed quiet came over the crowd as everyone's focus was on the two of us. While I was feeling like a skinned chicken in front of all these onlookers, Fargo seemed enlivened by the attention. His gait grew bouncier, his neck more strongly arched. I hoped I could borrow from his confidence.

As we rounded the corner toward the first fence, something shifted, and suddenly I was oblivious to all that surrounded us. We became aligned in a symphony all our own. First came the musical drumming sounds of collected hoof beats as we approached the first fence. Next the hefting sounds of horse and girl taking flight. Then the seemingly elongated suspension of time I always experienced when we soared through the air together. Followed by the landing thuds back on earth and the accompaniment of tinkling metal bit parts. These melodic measures were repeated over each fence. Our riding concerto concluded with the clicking of my own tongue as we hustled across the finish line. The sudden roaring applause at the end of our turn confirmed our first clean round together.

From that time forward, Fargo and I were an inseparable team. We competed in open jumping divisions along with the mega heights associated with the Gambler's Choice and Skyscraper classes. Graduating to the larger fences, navigating more complicated courses, and jumping for time turned out to be a good fit for both of us. I found the sensation of flying together endlessly exhilarating. I never grew tired of the adrenaline that infused my entire body when Fargo and I were in sync. My legs against his sides, the reins connecting his mouth to my hands, the energetic language flowing between us, girl to horse, horse to girl. By borrowing Fargo's strength, I felt stronger than myself, my lithe girl limitations becoming suddenly transformed as we together catapulted high up into the air. The surrendering, the soaring, the connecting. I knew even at the time that this would be an impossible experience to replicate in any other way. It was our own horse–girl love story. What more could I want? In these moments Fargo and I together seemed to have it all.

CHAPTER 23

IN THE STALL

The grooming process by a predator is often methodical. What was once experienced as a poke, with time, becomes merely the accepted norm. That is until the poke becomes a push, then a shove, then a . . . Up until that time, I thought that Clarentine and I had an implicit agreement that the limits had already been established . . . that is, until that late afternoon at the lower barn.

At fifteen, I was five years into the riding scene and an old hand. I knew how to ride and show horses, along with all the care and feeding. These never seemed like chores to me. And my body had grown strong through carrying buckets of water, stacking hay, shoveling manure, and pushing wheelbarrows. I reveled in feeling competent at these things and confident in my abilities. During this day's task of mucking out Jinx's stall, I was also drifting into my fantasies about the upcoming show. It's why I didn't see him coming.

With a pitchfork in my hand, wheelbarrow at the ready, and deep in thought, I suddenly saw Clarentine's shadow cast across the stall door. The horses had been put out to pasture, and the day had grown long. I hadn't noticed that everyone else had dispersed. I looked up as his presence intruded upon my reflective time. There he stood at the half stall door with his strong forearms casually folded across the top.

"Hey there, what are ya up to?"

There was something different in how he said this that snapped me to attention. He then unlatched the door and walked in before I could manage a response. I noticed that my movements became molasses-like even as my heartbeat raced. We now shared this enclosed wooden space, but I was standing at the back of the stall and he was blocking the door. In that moment I became acutely aware that stalls only have one exit.

My senses suddenly sharpened as I took in the smell of his working man perspiration and pungent cologne, the sound of his saccharine voice, the sudden feel of stifling air. I saw that the trap had been set for me.

"Just finishing up this stall before I take off," I answered as casually as I could muster.

He might have said something after this, but my body wasn't registering his words. Instead, tension was filling me from my guts clear to the outer seams of my tingling skin. I knew that it wasn't conversation he was after.

Time warped, for although it was only a matter of seconds, it seemed to stretch out in slow-motion frames that oozed forward as he quickly shortened the distance between us and grabbed me by my upper arms. The pitchfork I had been holding fell forward out of my grip as he crushed his bare-chested torso against my ribs, almost knocking the breath out of me. The weight of his body now lathered against mine, sandwiching me between him and the back wall of the stall.

At the same time, he smashed his open, wet mouth over mine, covering my face with his slobber and saliva. The vile taste of chewing tobacco and acrid bourbon invaded my mouth. His salacious tongue jammed deeper down my throat with urgency despite my feeble attempt to clench my jaw. I felt sure in that moment that I would drown under the weight and wet of him.

I struggled, twisted, and squirmed the best I could to get loose from his grip. I had always thought I could handle him and, even more delusional on my part, that I wouldn't have to. Feeling bruised and slimed and afraid of what might happen next . . . my survival reflexes kicked in. The surge of energy born of desperation unlocked some dormant strength to fight off this man who was far superior in size and stature.

Propelling my emboldened body forward, I managed to push him backward and slightly off-balance. Perhaps his fantasy that I would welcome his advances gave me the minuscule window I needed. Wrenching my arms free, I bolted out of that stall and ran for home.

At a safe distance up the hill, I tried to slow my panting breath and ease my body to a walk. My muscles ragged, my nerves jangled, I still couldn't quite take it all in. Resistance to the truth can act as a powerful sentry.

I was already in the process of reconstructing what had just happened. This was not a conscious deception on my part but rather an unconsciously protective one. I told myself that this, too, was manageable. I had gotten away, right? I told myself that underneath it all he cared about me. I even told myself that he respected me. I viewed myself as having some kind of special immunity. The alternative in that moment would have cast me as a victim. I couldn't afford to see myself in the starkness of that light.

I told myself a story that was consoling because I needed reassurance. It made this assault in the stall not so bad. This was just the price to pay for life at the barn, right? It is compelling for those influenced by abusive teachers, mentors, and coaches to create these adaptive narratives. Parents and guardians can fall into self-deception too. No one is eager to see what they don't want to be true.

How split I was from my true innards and the facts of my situation. Our capacity to rewrite history to avoid unmanageable pain is astounding. It is a useful coping mechanism to combat otherwise overwhelming feelings of helplessness. But because it requires an altering of reality, it also keeps us imprisoned and disconnected from ourselves and others. Life only happens in reality, so when we sever ourselves from the here and now, we also splinter off from the truth and our authentic response to it.

By the time I got to the house, this incident barely registered further than this. I told no one and no one asked why I was home before the dinner bell had rung. I returned to the barn the next day. While I kept my physical distance, both Clarentine and I pretended that nothing had happened. Nothing had happened, I told myself. Why would I want to make something of nothing? It was much more appealing to just try to forget it and move on, although the annoying poke had just become a shove.

CHAPTER 24

THE PROPOSITION

A few months after the incident in the stall, my friend Shannon foreshadowed another tempest on the horizon. She led me to a quiet part of the barn and with a hushed voice warned me, "Be careful, he's on the prowl."

In our world back then, it was rare that we riders ever spoke to each other about Clarentine's lecherous looks, forced kisses, or worse . . . He had separated and siloed us from talking about what was happening around us with each other. He had a lock on his environment along with everyone in it. Even when we girls were away from the barn at sleepovers, parties, or school, we muzzled ourselves into keeping up this level of misplaced loyalty. And yet, there was nothing cryptic in her words for me.

We had all grown accustomed to riding for "a horny old man." Everyone knew this about him: me, my riding friends, our mothers, the neighborhood, the town, the horse community. Never having married, he was always dating one or more women. He reveled far and wide in his ladies' man reputation. Some believed that this pertained just to adult females. However, we riders knew that this was only cover for his more heightened interest in the younger set. We had long since adapted around his predatory behavior with a cat-and-mouse dance. Making these adjustments was just the accepted conse-quence of riding for him.

Even so, Shannon told me that she'd noticed something different in his behavior lately. She proceeded to tell me that he tried to bribe her with all of it: entry fees paid at the upcoming shows, the chance to ride her favorite horse exclusively, new riding clothes—all for free if she just agreed to have sex with him. She felt an increased level of urgency behind his proposi-tion that she hadn't experienced before.

What struck me in that moment, even more than this rev-elation, was the fact that she was actually taking the time to warn me. No one I knew, with the exception of the mom who had phoned mine, had ever spoken out loud about this threat we were all constantly living under. Long before the term "whisper network" was coined, Shannon was doing just this: sounding the alarm and giving me a cautionary heads-up.

He didn't waste any time. It was only a few days later that Clarentine started a discussion with me about goals for the upcoming summer. At least, that was what I hoped we were talking about. He began by stating that he expected Fargo to do well in the open jumping division this show season and that he needed some fattening up to be ready to compete.

"Thought I'd keep him in a stall and throw the grain at him." He began weaving his web, then bored a look straight into me with a grin and slight tilt of his head for effect.

"That would be good," I responded while looking away and pretending I didn't understand what he might be implying. Meanwhile, my insides were being sandpapered.

"I'll let ya show him the whole summer too . . . for, ya know, doing it with me."

Although this was said in a euphemistic way, there was no doubt what he was asking. He was bargaining for me to have sex with him. Now my throat felt as dry as the dusty ground I was shakily standing on.

From the time Shannon had warned me, I imagined the speech I was going to give at this very moment. I fantasized that I would scold him for not thinking more of me than that. I craved his respect and admiration and thought that I could somehow argue my point and convince him to be who I wanted him to be and treat me how I wanted to be treated. What a false narrative I had created for myself!

At fifteen and in my already adapted denial, I couldn't grasp the intensity of his motives, the determination of his aims, or understand his predatory impulses. I still expected logic and reason to prevail. I couldn't see that I was only an object of his compulsive addiction. It was too much for my adoring girl-mind to accept that the "I" that I was trying to know and grow didn't even exist in his mind. So even though I had been preparing for this conversation, suddenly, all the air seemed to have abandoned my lungs. My fear hijacked my voice and I was unable to speak.

"Ya can decide when you want to," he offered up as if this sweetened the bargain. As if it was some generous compromise on his part.

"I don't want to," I eked out, my imagined speech crushed under the gravity of this moment.

His voice now took on that cloying quality as he moved slowly toward me like a hypnotic spellbinder. "There's nothing to worry about. I'll take care of everything. You won't get knocked up. It won't even hurt." His continued argument tightening like a vice grip.

Losing my virginity to him, the risk of pregnancy . . . I felt the disgusting ick factor. I didn't want to think about any of this. I didn't want to be in this position.

He might have taken my silence as a possible opening, for he cooed, "No one will ever need to know."

"That's not true," I reflexively spurted out with some new-found conviction in my voice. I knew about the circulating rumors beyond the barn, but even among ourselves we could be catty toward one another, speculating about who might be sleeping with him.

In a sterner voice, he used my response as a pivot for his next attack. "Everyone already thinks you're sleepin' with me, so what's the difference?"

Hearing it put so starkly stopped me cold. I couldn't argue with this. I had heard secondhand that some people did make assumptions about us, his riders, as if we were the seductive sirens that made it impossible for him to rein in his lust. On some level, I also bought into a misplaced sense that his appetite was somehow my fault, so his strategy in that moment—to stoke the shame and humiliation that already existed inside me—found its mark.

"No, I don't want to," I managed to say in a high-pitched voice that through my insecurity probably came out more like a comma.

"Maybe I'll just put Kate on Fargo then." Saving his biggest leveraged threat for last, he then said, "Or maybe I'll just sell him." It was a calculated low blow. Panic rose like a chicken bone suddenly lodged in my throat. I frantically tried to calm myself. *He wouldn't do that, would he? Fargo and I make the best team. He's my special show horse.*

There was a brief moment when I internally hemmed and hawed. Not out of ambivalence about having sex with him but out of my dread of the consequences of saying no, of making him mad, of losing Fargo and the opportunity to ride. This was the perpetual bind that I had been negotiating for years.

Even though I had been groomed to do everything he asked, on wobbly feet, I managed to turn and, without another word, stumble back up the hill toward home.

It never even crossed my mind to tell my parents. Why would I risk them taking me away from the horses that were such a big part of my life and source of my support? Why would I shoot myself in my own foot? *I got this*, I told myself with my now well-honed illusion of autonomy. As a teenage girl, thinking I could handle this situation—that I could protect myself—was equal parts grandiose and ignorant. In hindsight, I feel remorse about this narrative I told myself because it somehow placed me above those who were unable to withstand his oppression, his bribery, his persistence, his threats and abuse. As if we all weren't impacted by his reducing us into mere objects of his predatory gratification to be toyed with and coerced according to his desire.

Trying to piece it together years later, I believe that the fact that he relied on my parents' land for grazing his horses prevented me from experiencing even more pressure. This barter arrangement might have kept him from just forcefully taking what he wanted. I had this privilege, an unseen protection not afforded to others. Regardless, the horses grazed on our land while he continued to graze on me.

When we humans can't get out of a difficult situation, we often separate from our bodies and change the story. My version was to deactivate all negative emotions and continue to contort the narrative into believing that *everything was fine.* This fantasy helped temper the truth of being preyed upon, the truth of my acute vulnerability. This was my creative coping mechanism working overtime.

If I had been able to see this situation accurately at the time, I would have had to recognize myself as a victim. I would have had to accept a level of helplessness that felt intolerable. I also would have had to give up riding the horses I loved. I would have needed much more emotional support to do any of that.

My diary always served as a confidante for me. So later that night I wrote about this incident and his disturbing proposition. Rereading it decades later, there it was spelled out in my fifteen-year-old loopy handwriting: *He is persistent . . . I know he'll keep trying.* However, the scope of my understanding was so limited at the time and, by extension, my decision-making.

Across those confidentially lined pages, I continued writing my two-fold strategy like a secret manifesto. *I'll just not find myself alone with him . . .* was part one. It was condemning me to be even more vigilant as if adding more to my own burden was the solution.

The second declaration I wrote was, *I'll just have to ride my best ever.* That way, I concluded, *he will have to let me ride the horses that I most want to show even if I refuse to have sex with him.* On both counts, I thought that control and perfectionism would solve my predicament and maintain my relationship with the horses. Without saying it, I also assumed that it was possible to sidestep all consequences. This was the Faustian bargain I made as a girl. You know, the one with the devil.

CHAPTER 25

CONDITIONING

"You grew up in a cult!" Gary punctured through any remains of my false narrative with this statement during one session. I had never looked at my time under Clarentine's tutelage in this way before. At first I didn't want to hear how my therapist was defining the enormity of how I had been indoctrinated. It meant blasting open my otherwise shored-up version that I was somehow immune. But as we continued to tunnel into the influences of my past, I could see how my choices, my interpretations, my actions were all informed through the lens of this coercive environment.

What was presumed, I would now have to question. What I had once cobbled together was no longer coherent. Rather, it was the story I told myself to create a false sense of control. With my past experience at the barn now framed as a kind of cult, it was as if a previously missing key to the truth had been handed to me. It suddenly felt like my disjointed body parts were the tumblers of a previously locked safe finally clicking into open alignment.

Cult is the ultimate in conditioning. It is the extreme version of gaslighting. At its best, it operates from a doctrine based on humanitarian principles. At its worst, the intention is to create an atmosphere where abuse can take place undetected by the brain so that it seems to members that they have agency even while their choices are being eradicated from within.

As young girls of that era, we were already programmed by the culture to defer to strong authority figures, so we riders in this barnyard sect dutifully paid homage to our magnetic leader. He had corralled us into allegiance while we were heartfully communing with the horses.

Uncharacteristically, at the conclusion of that session, Gary assigned me homework. "Read about Charles Manson and the girls who were members of his deranged cult."

Yikes!

It was difficult turning those pages because some of the psychological similarities hit so close to home. A charismatic leader who is unquestioningly admired even though maliciously motivated—check. The absence of accountability to another authority—check. The use of tactics like shame, guilt, manipulation, and threat to get what the one in power wanted—check, check. There was another disturbing similarity: Charles Manson and Clarentine had both studied Dale Carnegie while in prison. Malevolent motivations can twist even well-meaning objectives to one's own ends.

Although my experience didn't fall into the strictest of definitions, the cultish part of these stables did not operate on ideology but purely from predation. Clarentine took advantage of the implanted chip in our naive hardware system.

We were all drinking the Kool-Aid back then.

Even poisonous Kool-Aid initially tastes sweet.

CHAPTER 26

GROOMED INTO DANGER

Having been subjected to a predator's intensifying desire since I was ten years old, I had become an adept acrobat. Trying to elude his advances was the norm that I pretzeled myself around daily. However, by the time I was sixteen, it was also a titillating surprise to discover that my gently developing curves were now captivating the interest of other males as well. This ability to turn attention in my direction was intoxicating. I found that my body offered me a sought-after currency, an elevated status that as a teenage girl I didn't otherwise have.

It was only later that I realized one byproduct of abuse is that these reflections become the constrictive glasses through which I viewed my own self-worth. There was no freedom to appreciate my own changing body or explore my own healthy sexuality on my terms when it was co-opted before I knew what was being sacrificed.

Clarentine's conditioning had effectively recalibrated my barometer reading, such that engaging in risky behavior no longer registered as dangerous. More than just the perils of jumping six-and-a-half-foot fences, I had a new proclivity for driving cars dangerously, misusing drugs and alcohol, and putting myself in compromising situations. It was as if I was compelled to seek out ways to play Russian roulette with danger.

My best friend at the time, Kelly, was two years my senior, owned a car, had parents who were passed out by dessert, and, like me, was one of Clarentine's stable of girls. The notion of potentially putting ourselves in harm's way was a shared blind spot. With my fake ID, courtesy of a mailing company, which passed muster with most door bouncers, we were regulars at the local bars on Saturday nights for dancing and drinking with guys.

This was the backdrop for how Kelly and I came to be at Easter Weekend, the biggest party of the year hosted by the frats at the University of Virginia in my hometown. The annual week of raucous activities culminated in the Saturday night joint kegger bash involving all of Greek row. Kelly and I weren't the only locals not wanting to miss out on the action.

That night, I remember wearing my white painter pants that were in style then. I had tied my lime-green V-necked sweater around my shoulders while my worn-in Docksider shoes capped off my outfit for the evening. Kelly sashayed in similarly preppy attire, fitting us deftly into the East Coast collegiate scene. Looking the part was our best cover.

I remember that we blasted music on the radio during our drive from the country into town while singing along to the hit songs "Play That Funky Music" and "Shake Your Booty" in anticipation of the fun night ahead.

The streets connecting frat row were already full of coeds holding plastic red and blue Solo cups by the time we arrived.

The frat houses had opened their doors, tapped the kegs on the lawns, and were booming their own music from large speakers placed in second-story windows or porch stoops. We helped ourselves to beer and blended right into the lively scene.

With free drinks and a chance to flirt with the college boys and dance in the warm spring evening air, it was easy to get caught up in the contagious atmosphere. I felt like I was a part of something bigger, something fun, something otherwise not available to me as a sophomore in high school. Naive despite my outward presentation, I didn't know that I was playing with fire. My experience at the barn left me an easy target.

I don't remember the exact moment of our meeting. Did he approach me? Did I talk with him first? Looking back, I didn't even know if he was a student there or a college boy who drove in from another campus to join the infamous party scene. The generous amounts of alcohol in my system acted like a gossamer cloth across my memory. I vaguely recall my hand in his, a grand set of sweeping stairs, the view of his back as he led me upward. Blond hair but no facial features. What prompted me to follow him? Then an empty room, a small bed, him closing the door. Did I protest? I can't remember, but I can't recall saying yes either. He probably didn't know that I was underage, but he must have known that I was drunk, terribly drunk. Then my mind blindfolded back onto itself, leaving only blackness, a blank void.

When I came to, I was alone, partially clothed, and lying on a mattress stained red. *Where am I? Is that my blood?* Then the awful stabs of some scraps of memory. How long had it been since I went upstairs? I didn't know. I stumbled dizzily to my feet, gained some tenuous balance, and walked gingerly out of the room. I looked down the large staircase onto the partying mayhem still going on below. I had no idea where Kelly was or how to find her. A backwash of fear was suddenly drowning me from within. I just wanted to go home. As I wandered the streets looking for my friend, I felt the added deluge of shame kick in. *Who had seen me? What were they thinking?* The humiliation doubled me over.

The external stain on that bed matched the internal stain I had already been carrying inside. *Wasn't what just happened supporting evidence for the accusations I felt from others?* I had internalized being one of "those girls." While Clarentine's reputation as a playboy was exalted, mine and all who rode for him seemed marked with our own brand of scarlet letters. Whether projection or truth, it felt like we, the victims, were being held responsible for what others didn't want to acknowledge or address. On some level, I felt plastered in shame, as if I was the cause of his exploitative behavior.

It was a relief when I finally found Kelly. I considered telling her what had happened, but my self-recrimination prevented me. *Didn't I ask for it? Hadn't I brought this night onto myself? These were the consequences of my choices, right?* This was my thinking at the time. Never mind that I was inebriated, unable to give informed consent—and was a minor. The way I framed this event canceled out these facts. It would never have occurred to me to consider it rape back then. And neither would the culture I grew up in.

We somehow located her car through the raucous crowd and navigated our way along the dark streets out of town toward home. Who knows how much she herself had drunk at that point. We certainly weren't thinking about one of us being a designated driver for the night.

After quietly sneaking into the house to avoid waking up my parents, I showered, sat on the toilet, and cried, amassing tears by myself with my parents fast asleep down the hall. I had no plans of ever telling them. What good would come from that? Unable to tolerate difficult situations and emotions, my mom might have even blamed me for what happened or erased it entirely. Her anxiety was always used as a weapon to silence my experiences. I took a shortcut and did this to myself first.

I decided that it was better that I just pretend it hadn't happened. An alternative to feeling like a victim is to feel responsible for what isn't ours to carry. So I curled up in bed alone that night, exiling my own pain. Imagined agency is a way to fend off helplessness, but shame thrives in unspoken secrets. If we are told messages directly or indirectly with enough repetition, then these lies take hold and begin reverberating from within our own heads as well.

When Clarentine propositioned me, I had said no. I continued to hold this position by the narrowest of margins. Because of this, I thought that I had avoided the impact of his predatory behavior. However, what I didn't see was that while I was saying no to him, I started to say yes everywhere else.

Through the rest of high school, I became even more rash, headstrong, and impulsive. Careless of all consequences for myself and others. I drove down long stretches of rural highways at a hundred miles per hour. I drank to excess, used drugs, and became "boy crazy." I can look back on this now and see the direct link to my having been sexually abused. But of course back then it remained invisible to me.

I was also juggling a double life. I got top grades, held leadership positions at school, and won championship ribbons at horse shows, so it all looked good from the outside. As long as I was externally successful, my parents believed everything was okay and left me alone. Long before the military coined it, my parents operated on a "don't ask, don't tell" basis. My external life reassured them that there was nothing to worry about. With their narrative intact, they could look the other way. Their lenient parenting certainly worked for my teenage self. Our bargain was a win-win. It saw me through the remainder of high school and my launch to college. I continued to ride for Clarentine on my breaks and whenever I was home in the summers.

CHAPTER 27

MURDER

I had just started my senior year in college six hundred miles from home when I heard that Clarentine had shot a man four times at close range inside the Ivy Store. The news of the local murder was disseminated throughout the community as rapidly as the gunfire itself. In retrospect, the surprising thing was not that Clarentine had killed for a third time but the fact that we all wholeheartedly supported him afterward.

The dead man turned out to be the husband and father of a mother-daughter duo who had been riding and boarding a horse at the barn. I didn't know either of them particularly well, but I had known other duos like them over the years. A vulnerable woman in need, easily seduced by Clarentine's charisma and his promise of companionship and protection. In this case, Clarentine was a place to vent her frustrations about her marriage and board her daughter's horse for free.

Piecing together the events from my riding friends, from the newspaper reports, and from Clarentine himself, I gathered that the two men had been trash-talking about each other long before the fatal incident at the convenience store. Their animosity for each other had been at a barely contained boiling-over point for some time. The other man hated that his estranged wife and daughter were hanging out with Clarentine, that his marriage might be over, and that this rumor was circulating around town.

Earlier that fated fall day, the cold war between them began to heat up when they ran into each other. They were both primed for a direct confrontation, and I can easily visualize Clarentine getting big in his stance like a tomcat who puffs up its body in preparation for a dark alley fight. I'd seen this before, how he would throw out his chest, stand imposingly taller, and deepen his voice to its most threatening bass pitch. He would have inevitably shortened the space between himself and his opponent. He knew how to dominate. He grew up fighting in the "holler" and was an offspring of a long-standing feuding family, so the combative, "never back down" legacy must have been surging in his veins.

I wonder if that man knew that Clarentine had killed twice before. Did he know that Clarentine had served prison time and was not deterred by facing this possibility again? Was he not intimidated by this man who towered over him in height and size? Did he really think he would convince Clarentine to stop spending time with his wife and daughter? Obviously there was no rational thought here on either side—only rampant testosterone, verbal threats, and a territorial dispute. In that moment, in that unassuming general store, the females were being verbally fought over like possessions, objects to go to war and ultimately to kill for.

However, the real tipping point came, as I heard it, when this other man disparaged Clarentine's mother. How interesting that it comes down to the reaction to some version of, "I'll make your mother wish you had never been born." These became the words that Clarentine felt were a necessity to revenge. These loyalties can be so deeply wired. Ironically, we riders were blindly devoted to him while he remained forever loyal to his mother.

As an aside, I never heard Clarentine talk about his father. This seems revealing in itself. Although I have no confirming facts, I imagine that he wasn't frugal with the belt, his fist, or the booze.

Clarentine countered this threat with one of his own. "If you ain't gone by the time I get back, you will regret it." In that moment, he threw down the gauntlet, leaving this ultimatum to hang in the air. With these last harbinger words, he got into the rickety truck and drove the mile-and-a-half stretch of road to the barn.

Clarentine later told me that back at the stables, he pulled out his .25 caliber automatic pistol. He proceeded to carefully clean and load it so it held a full round of bullets. Cocking the hammer, he strode over to the empty ring and practiced firing shots at the tin cans that sat on top of the rusty barrels, similar to the targets he'd set up for us when he taught us all how to shoot.

After having gotten in some practice, he then fed the horses and completed a few chores around the stables before getting into his truck and slowly driving back to the store. I wonder if the sputtering radio was playing Patsy Cline at the time or if he drove in silence. I wonder if he hoped that the man would be gone or still there. Most likely the latter. He gorged on conflict.

The man was still drinking coffee and grousing when Clarentine entered the store. As it was told to me, he then turned toward Clarentine, saying, "Did you bring your goddamn gun with you this time?" The accounts differ about what happened next but agree that it all happened fast. Clarentine drew his gun from his belt and fired. With this first bullet, the man fell to the floor on the spot. Clarentine proceeded to fire three more shots into his slumped body. Then without saying another word, he got in his truck and drove back to the barn and calmly waited for the police to arrive.

This wasn't an impulsive outburst of rage like I'd witnessed umpteen times before. This wasn't momentary madness from lack of frontal cortex access. No, this was something else. This was just, as Clarentine later stated, "what that man had a-coming if he hadn't left like he was told." His entitlement and rationalization for violence ran so deep.

Rather than this incident being a wake-up call to the cruelty we girls had been infused in, it instead further solidified our sense of allegiance. I flew home from college to find out firsthand what this would mean for Clarentine and how I could support him, the stables, and the horses.

CHAPTER 28

THE TRIAL

The fiercely debated point in Clarentine's trial hinged on whether this was a premeditated murder or manslaughter committed in the heat of anger. His lawyer recommended that Clarentine plead guilty, which, he asserted, would most likely reduce his sentence. Because Clarentine always thought he was innocent and right, he assumed that the consequences would be minimal. He expected to be released on probation. His arrogance always ran rampant.

After the hearing and out on bail, despite the prosecuting attorney's citing of his previous second-degree murder charges, Clarentine remained optimistic about the sentencing outcome. He continued to hold his own court back at the barn. I recall that he flaunted his brand of biblical humor as he recounted the event. "The Lord says 'seek and ye shall find,' well that man done 'sought and found' all right." Then smiling at his own cleverness, he'd recite his newest quip, "After saying my peace, I went and got my piece." In Clarentine's disturbed mind these were legitimate arguments.

I can't remember who organized our participation in his defense—was it his lawyer? One of the moms? Us girls?—but I was asked to write a letter of support on his behalf. I dutifully complied with this. I wanted to help in any way I could. I remember putting into empathetic words how he was an important mentor and teacher, how he gave us the opportunity to ride horses that was so crucial to our growth and development as girls and young women. How he was an upstanding citizen of the community. How much we all depended on him. How much we admired him.

The term "Stockholm syndrome" entered the limelight of my world back when I was fourteen. It was brought into the conversation when Patty Hearst was kidnapped from her college dorm room by a terrorist group. The abduction was dramatized by them to elicit media coverage attention and for the financial support that they hoped to garner by seizing the granddaughter of the famous and wealthy newspaper tycoon William Randolph Hearst. She was only nineteen. I was finishing middle school at the time and had already been under Clarentine's apprenticeship for four years.

But only a few months into this kidnapping, Patty was shown on film committing crimes alongside her assailants and was herself now also on the run from the law. The public debate about whether she could be held accountable for her actions began. Was she responsible for her decisions or had she been brainwashed into becoming one of them? The notion of Stockholm syndrome, the phenomenon where those being abused become unnaturally loyal to their abusers, became a heated topic. It spoke directly to the power of conditioning. Despite her defense's argument, she was found guilty, but the power of brainwashing was brought to the forefront.

We are all unconsciously shaped by the caretaking figures in our early lives and the values, messages, narratives, biases, and prejudices of not only our family systems but also from the communities and the culture in which we are raised. In the best of circumstances, we inherit positive experiences of healthy relating and the precious value of all sentient beings. Or it can be something entirely different.

While the infamous story of Patty Hearst's loyalty to her kidnappers inked the newspaper headlines in bold font, we young riders were quietly marinating in the conditioning taking place at our little off-the-grid stables. When does healthy conditioning cross the line into unhealthy brainwashing? Clarentine was calculating in his mind-bending techniques and charm. We weren't kidnapped. Our emotional hijacking happened slowly over many years. The protectively loyal bond that developed between him and us riders, despite the constant exposure to violence, sexual harassment, and abuse, had grown tenacious and strong.

This became blatantly apparent during Clarentine's trial. It is no surprise that the judge ended up with a stack of letters of support from us petitioning the judge to lessen Clarentine's sentence. Even though this wasn't a trial about sexual abuse charges, it wouldn't have mattered. Back then, only our allegiance bubbled to the surface.

If the circumstances were different and Clarentine was instead on trial today for his alleged predatory behavior toward us girls rather than the manslaughter charges, what would each of us choose to say? One might courageously speak out about Clarentine's unrelenting pressure to meet his sexual demands by leveraging her horse's need for safe harbor. His promise of "just once" turning into countless times. Another might share about the numbed dissociation she experienced each time he

sexually assaulted her. Another might describe the feeling of
the metal gun being put to her head when she threatened to
tell. These are only some of the ways I have since heard that he
subversively brandished his violent power.

Regrettably, at the time when we did have our day in court,
it wasn't for these charges, and we were still under the brainwashing influences that conditioned us to support, instead of
call out, our predator. Along with others, I testified through
my letter to the court on his behalf, my programmed fidelity to
him remaining seamless.

The case was declared second-degree murder rather than
the premeditated first-degree that the prosecuting attorney
had sought. Clarentine was initially given the maximum sentence of twenty years plus one extra year for having used a fire-
arm. Then, in the same breath, the judge suspended ten years
off that time. The leniency behind this decision was influenced
by us and reflected in the last paragraph of the local newspaper
article covering the trial. It read, *Clarentine had a fine reputation
in the community and was regarded as a surrogate father to many
children who boarded horses there.*

Although much less than the maximum charge, the results
were still devastating for us at the barn. What would become
of our beloved horses now? What would happen to the stables
in his absence? The judge gave him a week to get his business
in order.

CHAPTER 29

VISITING PRISON

By the time I next returned to Virginia, Clarentine's new address was at a rural state prison where he was serving an eleven-year sentence. My beloved Fargo had been sent out to pasture at a nearby farm. I was glad to hear that he would now be able to enjoy a carefree retirement plan. The other horses had also been sold or relocated to other farms. Ivy Creek Stables had been put in mothballs awaiting Clarentine's possible but uncertain return.

With Clarentine no longer down the hill at the barn, I felt compelled to go see for myself how he was managing his time in prison. After all, he had been my point of reference since I was ten years old. That misdirected compass was now pointing me toward a trip to visit him behind bars.

I was on schedule to graduate from college with a major in forensic studies. In my mind at the time, this presumed choice of what I studied in college was unconnected to my history at the barn. It never even occurred to me that the fact that my own childhood mentor was tried, sentenced, and serving time in prison for murder might have had something to do with my interest in the criminal system.

Denial is a useful adaptation until it isn't. The inherent dissidence that occurs when the mind tries to keep these overlapping facts neatly separate and compartmentalized is costly. It kept me unaware of what was motivating my actions in the world. It kept me cut off from myself and others. I was perpetuating the ability to fracture the emotions I inherited from both of my parental lineages as well. As a result, the past was still holding sway over me. My life wasn't yet my own.

Unconscious of all this, I borrowed the family station wagon to make the drive to the penitentiary. I had a large Virginia road atlas spread open on the passenger seat beside me. In that era before GPS, I had to stop occasionally and check the map to make sure that I was still going in the right direction. Clearly I wasn't.

As I drew closer to my destination, I passed a group of men working in the fields near the road. I had heard that Clarentine had been assigned to one of these chain gangs. Perhaps it was even this one. I inhaled deeply in preparation of seeing him. Was I there for approval? As support? Moth to the flame? At that time, I didn't understand my motives even though I blithely trusted them.

The screening procedure was not especially thorough back then, but even so, it felt invasive. I was checked for ID, questioned about who I was coming to visit, asked for signatures for liability and agreement to the protocol, patted down for whatever, then motioned on through when I was deemed not a risk. I was then guided down a narrow, industrial gray hallway that opened up to a partially covered courtyard area scattered with wooden picnic tables. The attempt to make it look casual was belied by the armed guards and surrounding chain-link fence.

I saw him off to one side as I entered. Even against this rigid background dotted with uniformed prisoners, he appeared as imposing and distinctive as ever. No one would mistake him in a lineup.

Smiling his golden smile, he motioned for me to join him at one of the tables. I had to lift my leg over the bench seat and sit directly across from him. It was a closer configuration than the distance I usually tried to keep between us. I was suddenly acutely aware that as a young woman, not only was I being watched and evaluated by those around me, but my mere presence here was going to bolster his reputation. I cringed with the discomfort of that realization. I was an objectified trophy for him once again.

Blocking out that gut hit for the moment, I asked him how he was doing. He told me that being in prison was no "big thang." He had been assigned to a work crew, where he labored much of his days in the fields clearing brush from the sides of the road with a group of other inmates. But he went on to affirm that he was used to heavy labor, was glad to be able to spend his days outside, and that, unlike when he was in prison before, they had new regulations that made life easier. They were now restricted from working when the heat surged above a certain temperature. They also were given more breaks, ate better food, and had access to TV.

He went on to tell me that he had already been promoted to prisoner foreman. Always a quick study in hierarchical survival, it didn't surprise me to hear he had figured out the way things worked, gained respect from his fellow prisoners, probably in part by intimidation, and was convinced that his sentence would be shortened when he came up for a parole hearing in three and a half years.

Then our talk turned to the barn. He asked what I had heard from the others, what I knew about the horses. It was then that I found out others had also been to visit him. He was more informed than I had been while away at college. I felt a flutter of that old jealousy, the competition between us girls for his attention. Funny how that desire to be special in his eyes still had its tentacles in me.

He said that his overall goal was to look better when he got out than when he went in. His strategy included staying in shape, trimming off some pounds, and using linseed oil on his hair and skin. It was odd to hear him speak so directly to his vanity.

I later found out that while in prison, he had reconnected with an unrequited love interest he knew from his past. She was recently widowed and his sister put them back in touch. Turns out he would have a new girlfriend even before his release from prison. His spell-casting ways weren't deterred by iron bars.

Although it wouldn't be the very last time I saw him, driving away from the prison that day, I knew that I wouldn't be going back there again to visit him. The veil across my vision was beginning to thin. I was starting to see my own metal bars and my lack of freedom from this man. His spell on me was weakening. As I saw the need for distance from him, I also knew that I had to sever my equestrian ties. At the time, horses and Clarentine were too inextricably linked. For my emotional well-being, I had to jettison both.

CHAPTER 30

THE LETTER

Having finished college at twenty-two, I moved across the country to Seattle, sight unseen, to start a master's program in clinical social work. Over the next decade, I worked in different settings as a psychotherapist and built a life in the Pacific Northwest. Mark and I met and married, purchased a home outside Seattle, and became parents. I knew that I had further untangling to do, but seeing exactly how my past might be constricting my adult life was still strangely elusive.

By then it had been twelve years since I had been one of Clarentine's riders, but even so, during a trip back to Charlottesville when I was in my early thirties, I impulsively ventured to the barn to see him again. He was out of prison, released early on "good behavior," and running his stables anew with a different crop of girls and horses by his side. My old, unhealthy emotional attachment to him led me to greet him warmly, banter casually, and listen to his latest stories. My once adaptive splitting had mostly kept my inward response to him siphoned off from my awareness, but now I felt the anxiety contract my insides like the wringing of a wet rag. I was feeling the unacknowledged reverberations of his abuse in my body on a visceral level. It took this visit for me to realize that by having contact with him again, I was allowing him to maintain a chokehold on my life.

After this visit to the barn, it became clear that I couldn't explore the impacts this man had had on my life without first creating emotional room for myself. Around that same time, Mark and I started couples therapy with Gary, and it was with this help back in my early thirties that I first began to deconstruct my past.

With this in mind, Gary proposed that I write Clarentine a letter ending all contact with him. After all, real change requires taking concrete actions. This idea gave me an immediate sense of relief, but teetering on the brink of closing this door once and for all, I hesitated. The fact was that I also loved Clarentine. Despite it all, I still held a place for him in my heart.

Love is one of the strongest emotions. It sounds so crazy in retrospect, but I adored him. It is confusing when mentor and abuser are the same person. I had written testimonials on his behalf, condoned his actions, accepted his guidance. It is hard to be angry at someone you've been groomed to love. Much easier to be self-blaming and self-negating.

When the wiring is all backward, then the natural impulses and the means of seeing the situation for what it is become limited. It makes the emotional circuitry go haywire. For another thing, it messes with the ability to self-protect and accurately self-narrate. These paradoxical emotions and impacts are some of the elements embedded in complex trauma.

However, one of the qualities that makes us human is our capacity to experience conflicting emotions at the same time. Love and anger, grief and rage, despair and hope. The problem occurs when we assume feelings must be binary. "I feel this; therefore, I can't feel that." Under those circumstances, one feeling must nullify the others. This comes at the detriment of expressing our authentic, whole selves. The fact is our feelings are often messy and overlapping.

What had taken me decades to realize is that the love I felt for Clarentine had little to do with him and everything to do with me. I was capable of loving. I was innately geared toward giving my heartfelt affection to another human being. Just because I didn't have the perspective to distinguish who deserved this or not didn't make it my fault for loving him.

Ironically, but in a very different way, while he was objectifying me, I was also objectifying him. In one of my childhood journals I referred to him as "my moral-less saint." That summed up how, as a girl, I placed him on an admirer's pedestal and rationalized away any accountability for his despicable actions.

He, on the other hand, co-opted and exploited this emotional bond I innocently gave for his own purposes. It was the underlying tendon of power that tethered me close to him. With his diagnosable charisma, along with my love for horses, he kept me in a bewitched trance.

Through my childhood eyes, he embodied attributes that were attractive—he was powerful, protective, and confident. What I couldn't see behind that veneer was that these were masks for dominant, possessive, and narcissistic. I wanted to feel loved. I wanted to be seen. I could not differentiate this from being objectified. My adoration was in good faith, but this becomes a predator's treasure trove.

When I did sit down to put words to paper, I quickly realized that my first draft sounded like a "Dear John" letter.

Through the reflection on the page, I saw more clearly how he had, over the course of years, sexualized me into a mistress, one of many in his horse-riding harem. I could more acutely see that severing all contact would begin a process of reclaiming myself. This letter gave me the means to finally say, "Enough."

Finding my voice through my written words, I confronted him about his abusive behavior and the impact it had exerted over my life from the time I was a young girl. I made it clear that this would be the last time he would ever hear from me. And it was. I learned that he died ten years later.

I assume that he received the letter, but it didn't matter. I had spoken my truth and taken back control of my life. I regret that I also didn't report him to any authorities at the time when I was first breaking away from his emotional grasp in 1994. It wouldn't be until 2017 that a new resource called SafeSport would be formed to oversee the protection of young athletes who are inherently in a power imbalance with their coaches and trainers. This organization is now committed to investigating complaints of abuse and advocating on behalf of those who are vulnerable. However, back when I left the barn for good, there was no such means to lodge a complaint. With the long-armed conditioning of silence still keeping me separate from a sense of community, I left without looking back as to who else might still be caught in his tractor beam. I feel deep remorse about this now.

Getting in touch with the full force of my anger would require more layers of shoveling, but this initial step gave me space to inhale. I hadn't realized until then all the ways that I had been holding my breath.

CHAPTER 31

KALI AND MY
MISSING ANGER

I t was within this newly formed boundary that Gary asked, not for the first time, "So where is your anger at Clarentine?" I again noted my numbness in the face of this important question. My disconnect meant that I had to do an all-out archaeological dig of those feelings that I knew I must be carrying. How could I not be angry? All those years of grooming, the ways he made me feel so self-conscious in my own skin, his sexual assaults, his violent behavior . . . It illustrated the extent of my emotional imprisonment that I had to go in search for these feelings toward my abuser. However, he wasn't the only factor dousing my authentic feelings. I had absorbed plenty of internalized taboos about anger from others too.

In college, along with my sociology and psychology courses, I studied comparative religion. I appreciated learning about the Hindu pantheon, but Kali, the goddess of destruction, didn't start out as my favorite—that is, until she became my superpower. From my first impressions, she was just "too much" of everything—too fierce, too ravaging, too intense.

She carried too many skulls at her hips and waved too many arms. Her role is to raze everything to the ground, after all.

Growing up around my conservative mother, anger, like spitting in public, just wasn't becoming for girls. The traditional message for what constituted acceptable emotions for women was, and still largely is, so narrowly defined: be nice, be kind, be compliant, be a peacemaker, be a caregiver. The expression of anger comes with consequences. It certainly wasn't what girls who were conditioned to seek approval were allowed to share. The poor antidote offered was to "just forget about it." If anger persisted, it was met with, "Why can't you just get over it and move on?" and "What's wrong with you that you can't?"

Ironically, this disowned feeling was exactly what I had always needed. How can we become who we are if we get emotionally handcuffed from the start? How the hell can we protect ourselves? Anger is, after all, an authentic response to injustice. It is a necessary element for standing for one's integrity, fighting for one's and others' rights, setting boundaries, taking action. The cultural conditioning against anger contributed to my being easy prey. I was like a declawed cat sent out into a world of junkyard dogs.

In addition to the messages from this larger context was my lived experience where anger became associated with danger. Clarentine's version showed up as unpredictable, violent rage. Repressing my own anger against him was a matter of safety. My mother was also impulsive and hurtful when I attempted to express my anger. She would suppress me by shouting me down, slapping my face, running from the room. Anger ricocheted back toward me in the form of punishment, retribution, or a withdrawal of love.

Never having witnessed any good coming from anger, I didn't see any value in feeling my own. So initially, unearthing my anger was like locating a missing horseshoe thrown into a grassy meadow. I knew that it was there, but everything protective in me avoided it. I didn't want to associate with that emotion. I instead coupled it with bad things—bad behavior, bad consequences, bad breath—as in fire-breathing dragon breath. My own anger felt like I wasn't in control and was sure to be rejected.

By attempting to distance myself from my anger, I only created a crevasse within myself. I had become a castaway from my own experience. And the problem with anger is it doesn't just go away. With a long half-life, it seethes and festers and inevitably comes out sideways. I knew from the work I had done on my marriage that my repressed anger had seeped out under the guise of resentment, contempt, and criticism. My anger was operating—just covertly.

In order to explore my anger in a therapy session one day, I was guided back into a particular scene from the past. I saw the stables, the tack area, and Clarentine striding angrily toward Little Light. I could suddenly envision all over again how the rage contorted his face. I saw him swing the twitch up in the air. I saw the panic in this small pony's eyes as she desperately tried to escape the impending blow. I watched again in horror as he began to beat her into submission while she pulled against the fence, fighting for her freedom with all she had.

Reconjuring up this scene, I felt the helplessness drench me again. I had been programmed to be passively complicit in his violence. For years! Was I even capable of stopping him now? Now, from my adult self? How do we learn to act through our protective paralysis? Even when it only existed here in my own imaginings, this felt daunting.

I pictured myself trying to push him away from her buckskin body and instead saw him grab me by my wrist and throw me to the ground. I pictured him laughing as he stood over me. "Who do you think you are? You can't fight me. I will crush you."

The long-held smoldering pile of ash in my belly suddenly ignited. From deep within, I felt Kali emerge through me. He needed to be stopped, and I needed to resurrect my rightful anger in order to do it.

"*No more!*" I shouted and affirmed to myself. "*I no longer relinquish my power to those who want to control or hurt me—or others.*" I felt the plug of energy release with a surge. In my mind's eye, I raise up my imagined sword. I swing this gleaming metal through the air and slash off his right arm. *No more hitting!* Then *whoosh, slice,* I cut off his left. He had beaten too many horses and abused too many girls with those arms. *Never again!* Like a machete bushwhacking through dense underbrush in order to clear a trail, I then wield my weapon to chop off his legs.

I pause and take a breath before my culminating blow. As I pendulum the sword in a downward arc, I sever his head cleanly from the rest of his body. Strangely, I feel my body re-aligning as I dissect his. It's ironic that the thing we avoid the most holds the very power to deliver us back to ourselves. My righteous anger was enlivening me.

Charged with this newly released vitality, I now imagined shoveling his parts into that rusty, old wheelbarrow. I had rolled many a load of manure and hay and grain in that heavy metal contraption throughout my youth. Now I visualize myself scooping up his remains into that same wheelbarrow and rolling him to the lower barn. As I upend him, I watch his arms, legs, and torso slide to the ground. His head rolls out last like an exclamation point at the end of a declarative sentence.

I have no regret for cutting him limb to limb in my fantasy. My anger at him is just, but at the same time, I am no murderer. He is already dead—I am but vanquishing his hold over me. I am victorious, not in his dominating way, but as a destroyer of what is toxic, as a protector of what is sacred. By channeling my inner Kali, I am also destroying the delusions and distortions that I have been carrying about myself and this situation for far too long. I am winning the fight to reclaim my own truth.

But . . . not so fast. I also loved him.

Spontaneously, I bend down and tuck loose hay around his piled-up body parts. My care for him was always evidence of my humanity. Kali, for all her fire and destruction, is also the goddess of compassion. She represents the ultimate in both/and—she offers a magnitude of necessary abolishing as well as much-needed empathy for the world. When I embraced this paradox, I found I wasn't scorched by the raging fires after all. In fact, when I stopped running from my anger, I also narrowed my distance with intimacy. Kali teaches that we can only be truly caring if we are able to experience the full continuum of our authentic emotions. This is what makes us human. This is what connects us to each other.

I contend that Kali is everyone's superpower. A version of her resides within us all and is ready when needed because not only do we need to demolish the forces propping up inequities of all kinds, but we also sometimes have to raze our own inner demons to the ground in order to fight for our freedom and the freedom of others. Over and over again.

CHAPTER 32

THE TALK

N ow that I had sent my letter to Clarentine and had given myself an opportunity to feel through my experience of him, it became obvious that there was another place that I had left unaddressed. I was in my thirties and hadn't yet talked directly to my parents about what had happened to me during all those years of riding. I recognized that my silence only served to perpetuate my internalized narrative that what happened to me was all mine to shoulder.

Had I been waiting for them to ask me about my years at the barn? There it was, a lingering wish to be seen and acknowledged. Instead of giving them the power to release me, it was time for me to proactively validate my own experience out loud and liberate myself from this unspoken secret.

They were coming to Seattle for a visit. The time was ripe for this conversation, so I gave them a heads-up that I had things from the past that I wanted to discuss. It was awkward and formal when we all took seats around our small living room on that agreed-upon evening. My mother sat in an upright chair while my father slumped casually onto the couch. Mark was also there for moral support. I had never talked about my experience at the barn with my parents before. I felt more acutely the chasm this was creating between us. It had become too burdensome for me to continue to carry this in silence.

Now that we were all gathered, though, every cell in me was screaming, *What are you doing? Don't!* It was gut-wrenching to stand on the threshold of going against the grain by speaking my long-held-back truth. This is the emotional rub: to show up differently is to change the entrenched system that is invested in keeping it all the same. This elicited in me feelings of guilt and betrayal. Misplaced loyalty to the status quo can easily cut us off at the knees.

I kept reminding myself that speaking honestly and openly was a commitment to myself. By naming and facing my past victimhood, I could better reconnect with myself and others, but my underarms burst out in a sweaty show of resistance and my throat tightened in opposition against the truth leaking out. To dare to speak about what I had up until that time chosen to stay quiet about went against all the cellular messages to not rock the boat, but I knew that this was the moment to advocate for myself.

I was coming to understand that although it didn't feel like it, speaking up was also a commitment to my parents. It would give them a chance to hear me, respond to my hurts, and participate in the possibility of healing these old rifts between us. So I drew up the courage to be transparent and vulnerably began.

My awkward words started with a stutter then surged forth like I was dislodging a hairball. I told them that through the years, Clarentine had ogled me, leered at me, grabbed me, had forced me to kiss him, and had pressured me to have sex with him. I told them that this was my daily experience for nearly as long as I could remember.

My mother gasped. She drew in this fearful breath like she had just seen a terrifying monster jump out of the corner of the room. Her face seemed to register in that first flush the horrific entirety of what I was revealing and what she had always feared. This involuntary response would be her most authentic. The room barely held that weighty pause because here lay the potential for so much to transform between us.

However, with the rawness of my words still swirling in the air, she just as quickly snapped it all shut. "That can't be true. He always had a girlfriend." This response doubled back and hit me square in the face. Having a steady girlfriend meant that the story of his constant flirtation stopped there. The fact that he was always dating someone added to his credibility and gave him just the alibi he needed. In addition, my mother was always a brutal editor when her comfortable narrative was at stake.

I pushed forward challenging them both for not seeing, for not wanting to see, the dangerous situation that I had been in since the time I was ten years old. I shared my pain that they hadn't been there emotionally for me, hadn't protected me, hadn't recognized the loneliness I felt as a result. I had had to navigate it all alone.

For me it boiled down to, "Why didn't you protect me?" I wasn't asking this to blame them. It was because I no longer wanted to carry the burden of that responsibility. I needed to release the weight of the accompanying shame that I had been plagued by for too long.

My mom didn't miss a defensive beat. "We could never have stopped you from going down to the barn. You were stubborn and defiant. What could we do? You wouldn't have listened to us anyway."

Ah, here it was. The source of my own self-incrimination and my mom's abdicating of her own responsibility to parent me. I had regularly been accused of being selfish, stubborn, too independent . . . The list went on. It was implied now that because of this, it was my fault that they couldn't step in and keep me safe.

I had also internalized this same belief that I was to blame for all that had happened, that I somehow had chosen it. I also carried the regret of not speaking up on behalf of others. My silence acted as complicit support of him. And I did love the horses. I wanted to spend all my time at the barn. I would have balked if they had tried to stop me . . . But I was a kid. I couldn't possibly see the larger ramifications. Back then, I couldn't have set my own protective boundaries.

I needed them, as my parents, to see this for me, to see that I was in over my head. I needed them to extricate me from that situation—kicking and screaming if necessary. But they weren't that committed to taking a strong position on my behalf. Neither one of them would have been able to withstand my disappointment or my anger. It became convenient for them to feel powerless over my desires.

"Did he ever . . . you know?" murmured my mother.

"No, but . . ." My words trailed off in the deflation I suddenly felt. Here was the point in the charged discussion that I was thwarted by my own narrow definition of sexual abuse back then. In my own mind at the time, I doubted the seriousness of my experiences because he hadn't what? Forced me to engage in intercourse or oral sex with him? At that point, I was still minimizing what had happened.

The cultural views on this subject provided no support. I had finished graduate school in social work, accepted a job in a mental health agency, and started seeing clients all before the Diagnostic and Statistical Manual even offered a limited definition of sexual abuse against minors that didn't include the continuum of grooming. According to this, I had perhaps been harassed but definitely not "sexually abused."

Back then, the definition was hamstrung by the same lack of consciousness that existed in society. It was a product of a culture that couldn't yet acknowledge or talk openly about what was tragically happening in camouflage for so many young girls—and boys too. By extension, the laws were constructed out of these same biases and limitations. We can only heal what we can name. This obstruction of the truth meant that the impact on me was also cloaked.

Since that time, the definition of sexual abuse has broadened to include exploitation through all forms of sexual actions or even suggestions of sexual actions in the context where one person holds power over another. But this more enlightened and enlarged definition was still decades away.

Back in my living room, the air seemed suddenly thin. There remained a shroud obscuring the fact that I—and many of my friends—had been sexually abused by a calculating predator.

In a feeble attempt to strengthen my wilting case in the face of my mother's dismissive responses, I started sharing some of what I knew to be the harsher assaults that a friend had experienced at the barn. My own abuse didn't seem credible enough, so I used her story in my plea for my parents' concern. I was becoming desperate.

I knew that Clarentine had forced her into having sex with him. I shared some of what I knew. What I didn't know until much later were details about some of the other heart-wrenching and terrifying stories my riding friends endured.

I feel remorse when I reflect back now to think that I co-opted my friend's experience to try to give credence to my own. In my misplaced effort to get my parents to understand, accept, and affirm the seriousness of his impact on me through the years, I misappropriated someone else's trauma. I deeply regret this.

I thought that if they only heard the truth, then they would be able to actually see me in this way, confirm what I had lived through, empathize with the bind I had been in, and genuinely apologize in some way. My hope was that sharing my truth would end our collusion of denial so we could move forward in a renewed way.

My idealized mother would have heard my pain and anguish. She would have seen that it was courageous of me to talk about what I had been carrying alone for so long. She would have been able to tolerate her own pain enough to hear mine. She would have admitted that she knew the barn was a dangerous situation and that she never stopped long enough to take action to keep me safe from him. Out of this recognition, she would have been able to genuinely say she was sorry and feel the weight of her complicity in my abuse. She would have validated that she loved me and told me I was brave to bring it up. She wouldn't want me to feel alone anymore. She would have hoped that someday I would forgive her but, in the meantime, would vow to remain open to talking about it whenever I needed to bring it up. She would commit to getting help so that she could learn to be less consumed by her anxiety and more emotionally available.

This is what I would have loved to hear. This would have felt healing. As it turned out, this hoped-for outcome was relegated to fantasy. Instead, my mother expressed nothing other than what emerged as a series of gravelly clicking sounds while she worried her hands together, fussed with her collar, and sped hastily from the room.

My father stayed behind. He did tell me he loved me and was sorry for all that happened. I am grateful to him for this. Because he could at times show up emotionally, he was always easier to love and forgive.

However, my idealized father would have been able to recognize that his passivity was also a form of violence against me. He prioritized his own comfort and a false harmony in our household over the truth and looked the other way both when it came to my mother and Clarentine. By not challenging my mother's behavior, he also abdicated his parenting responsibilities and failed to protect me. He avoided conflict at my expense.

The next day, my mother came into the room where I was sitting. She remained standing, and her straight-backed, rigid posture conveyed to me that this wasn't going to go well. Like a robotic emissary delivering a declarative message, she pronounced that my riding friend was lying and the accounts I had heard were exaggerations. Then without waiting for my response, she turned and strode back out of the room and out of the house.

I felt sucker-punched. I should have seen it coming, but I hadn't. The bit of remaining air, along with the hope in me, vaporized in an instant. She all but said directly that she didn't believe me and insinuated that I was a liar.

It was shocking to hear her in one statement so efficiently annihilate my experience and me along with it. According to her, it never even happened. But I realize that this lay at the very core of what I had experienced all my life. Staying in control was everything to her. She often needed to dismiss me because of it. Now, with this large truth-telling, she had to make me and my feelings completely disappear. It required a full-fledged evisceration.

This was her attempt to put it all back in Pandora's box. Her drawn conclusion was all that stood between her holding it together and completely falling apart. The problem is that this narrative she created didn't have me in it.

There were no words or energy left to argue. Even if I could have formulated a response, now in the wake of an empty room, there was no one to say it to. Along with the impact of abuse, I would need to grieve and shed the fantasy of the mother I wished I had had.

It was a double betrayal—not protected, then not believed.

The sliver of a silver lining in this awful interaction was that it was actually validating—just not in the hoped-for way. It confirmed that my mother was only ever capable of hearing what she could tolerate. She categorically dismissed and denied all that didn't fit into her comfortable schema. Here was proof of why I found it so hard to share with her and why I felt I had to manage it by myself. Recognizing my mother's limitations—my father's too—during this pinnacle weekend helped me understand that she was never capable of being a resource for me. She was too busy repressing her own anxieties.

In preparing to have this conversation, I had shared with Mark my worst-case fear. I worried that my truth would literally kill my mother. This seemed almost to come to pass. Soon after my exchange with her, she experienced serious chest palpitations and was rushed to the hospital for tests. Panic attacks can feel like one is experiencing a deadly heart attack. We never spoke of any of it again. My mom wasn't malicious or cold-hearted. She was just too wrought with anxiety to tolerate her emotions, let alone mine.

Making the unconscious conscious can be agonizing. The default feature of all our internal resources is set to protect us from just such pain. This intrinsic capacity to deny difficult truths is strong. I don't harbor blame for this because I see how this has operated in my own life. I appreciate how challenging it is to exchange fiction for fact. The choice then becomes opening ourselves to new actions informed by this awareness or holding tight to a comfortably distorted narrative.

Through this difficult interaction, it became crystal clear that I couldn't expect my parents to confirm my experience or even accept it. But by giving myself permission to speak up, set boundaries, and off-load what wasn't mine to carry, I had honored my own experience. I came to see that these limitations were theirs, absorbed through the generations.

Following this, I took a break in contact with my parents to give myself the space to grieve the fact that I didn't and wouldn't get what I emotionally needed from either of them. It is hard to not be attached to that. Yet I knew that holding on to any hope that they might change would only continue to fuel my disappointment and resentment. Coming to accept their limitations was now the choice I had before me. I was also realizing that as an adult, I no longer needed their validation or approval. My work moving forward from here was my own responsibility.

With time, I re-engaged with them and ultimately came to forgive and love my mom, not from a place of obligation or the well-oiled impulse to pander to her, but for the person she was and the ways that she also had been shaped and fractured in her life.

CHAPTER 33

THE LINGERING RESIDUES OF TRAUMA

When I was a girl, playing on the playground but not impersonating a horse, there was a game of folding paper into a design that became a handheld oracle of sorts. After stating a question, my girlfriends and I would take turns putting our thumbs and pointer fingers inside the four main folds. Then we would snap the origami-like paper gadget in different directions to a singsongy rhythmic chant. When the song stopped, it revealed a triangle of paper. The answers to our heartfelt questions were hidden under these unassuming flaps.

We are all metaphoric versions of this: made up of concealed folds that hold both the buried traumas and the answers to our innermost questions, but it inevitably involves an ongoing process of flip-flopping around as we continue to open and close to the truth about ourselves and what has shaped us.

Back then, in my thirties, I clung to the appealing narrative that went something like: *Now that I have taken the time to dig through these layers of my childhood and set boundaries as a result, I should be done with the past.* After all, I had written Clarentine a letter ending all contact. I had confronted my parents about the lack of protection and support that I experienced from them. It hadn't gone as I had hoped, but that wasn't the point. I had taken the actions that were within my control. I had spoken my truth and shifted something within myself by doing so. I thought that meant the past was, well, in the past.

We are compelled to want the difficult stuff to be behind us. Despite those wishes, old traumas can cause the mind and body to respond otherwise. I disassociated from my feelings about Clarentine's abuse back at the time, and yet a slammed door or an unexpected touch on my shoulder can elicit a disproportionate flood of pent-up reactivity.

It can be a confusing experience when these spikes of adrenaline come sprinting out of the past unannounced. When we find ourselves suddenly awash with anxiety, racing heartbeats, sweating . . . it is confounding. *Why is this happening now? Why am I suddenly overwrought in this mundane situation? Why does this feel worse than it ever did back then?* The fact is PTSD (post-traumatic stress disorder) in the present can feel as disruptive or even more so than what has already been lived through. It is shown that the memories of happy events and joyous occasions aren't absorbed with the same detailed sensations throughout the body as the traumatic events are. In other words, trauma takes up much more bandwidth.

Our bodies are elaborate storage systems with long-term memories. Trauma gets archived. When the internal replay button activates the vagal nerve that runs the length of the internal body, we can experience an emotional overload, which turns our parasympathetic calm into a sympathetic hyperdrive state. Once the nervous system is fired up, it is difficult to stop the involuntary reactions that plunge our bodies into survival mode. The problem is not that the body holds our trauma on a visceral level. The difficulty is that the body can't tell time.

My own dormant cells have accumulated years of Clarentine's yelling, hitting, cursing, grabbing, invading . . . into my young girl-body receptacle, both as a target and as a witness to violence. These feelings have quietly hibernated in refrigeration for decades. For me, the portals into the past can be activated by unexpected loud sounds and objects moving toward me or situations involving performance like competitive sports events. These circumstances can elicit an internal panic that suddenly rampages my nervous system.

Once, when a flung squash racquet from my friendly opponent careened in my direction, I instantaneously began hyperventilating and found myself unable to catch my breath or speak through my bolting heartbeats. Other times, the triggered experience feels like I'm attempting to wade through thick molasses with heavy limbs and eyes that are unable to focus. Sometimes it's momentary, and a handful of times, these symptoms were protracted and left me deeply shaken. During these particular flash points, the past has retroactively become superimposed onto the present. In these moments, my body has time-traveled.

I have come to view these reactive experiences as validation of how difficult being around a raging, alcoholic pedophile had actually been for me back in the day. I dissociated so that I wouldn't feel the full impact of that then, a useful coping mechanism, but meanwhile, my body was nevertheless logging the experience for me. Now these same bits of trauma, held in my body, can dislodge and cause havoc on my system, reminding me of what I have already lived through.

These challenging reverberations tell our story. Knowing this can help us have empathy for the self-protective mechanisms that were unconsciously installed once upon a time when we were barraged with overwhelming emotions and experiences we couldn't contextualize.

Although these re-amplified situations come uninvited, I now choose to see them as emissaries, not enemies. Damn, it isn't what we want, but if we can welcome it anyway, then we can stop fighting against ourselves, choose to befriend these fears and anxieties, and replace negative judgment with self-compassion.

In these times, we also have to remember that feeling intense stress doesn't automatically mean that we are unsafe. This reactivity and our conditioned responses most often come from the past, not from the present situation. Change is inherently unpleasant, so any activating trigger can lead our bodies to respond as if we are in danger when we most likely are not.

However, sometimes a body's vigilance is absolutely warranted. There are many people who are continually and chronically under the real threat of marginalization, discrimination, and violence in our culture. For those of us who have the privilege of relative safety, it is imperative to do the work to be able to discern the differences between *unsafe* and just *uncomfortable*, even if stemming from a traumatizing past. Otherwise, whenever confronted with a chance to learn about ourselves—which also benefits the world—we will tend to keep doubling down on our imagined victimhood. Confusing the lack of agency that we had as children with ourselves as powerful adults now is its own form of aggression. Bringing curiosity to these situations can help slow down habitual patterns. Learning to distinguish between what's coming from the past and what's in the present prevents us from squandering the opportunity for growth and connection. Trauma informs our lives, but it doesn't define or need to limit us.

When we experience echoes from the past, there are ways to help re-regulate a system thrown out of whack. Our bodies are geared for motion, especially when under perceived duress, so deep breathing, energetic physical movement, and even dunking in ice water at times of high activation can be especially helpful. A general self-soothing practice could include tapping, yoga, qigong, sitting and walking meditations . . . to name only a few of the many available resources.

For me, crafting mosaics is also part of my emotional tool kit. I find—and brain research concurs—that connecting broken pieces into a whole (like putting together puzzles) becomes more than only metaphoric in its healing. It offers an integrating, relaxing, hands-on experience that is not thinking-based. Of course, being in a community with others can't be overestimated. Connection is key to our ability to self-regulate and our overall well-being as humans. Customizing a supportive mind-body-social-spiritual practice is what's needed for the courage it takes to be on this journey called life.

The goal of trauma work is freedom. Not necessarily from the pain or the nervous system's reflexive response but from our own misinterpretations of what happened to us. For me, it is the work of lining up fully with the reality of the abuse I had been chronically exposed to and questioning the once intractable story I told myself as a result. My narrative—that it wasn't so bad, that there were no long-term consequences, and that I was over it now anyway—was keeping me in a blind alley. I couldn't see that this is what made it difficult for me to connect to my own emotions, ask for help, and trust that others wanted to be there for me.

The problem when we unconsciously create inaccurate narratives about what happens to us is two-fold. We can end up taking on responsibility for circumstances beyond our control, and we can split off from our own authentic feelings. Carrying the blame for what was never ours to carry leads to shame, guilt, and humiliation. Suppressing our emotions leads to a distorted sense of self, isolation, and, as I saw in myself, the common tendency to unconsciously inflict harm on others.

Like an invisible undertow, it was hard to see how the messages I absorbed and the narratives I constructed were covertly operating. The break in my marriage, twenty years later, painfully exposed some of these unaddressed currents and what I had been negatively paying forward.

CHAPTER 34

RECONCILING MY MARRIAGE

Four months had now passed since I had been out of the house and with it, much introspection. Through having to live alone for the first time in more than twenty years, I could see how what Gary called my "hostile dependency" had been affecting our relationship. I took for granted the ways that I had become needy while at the same time begrudged my reliance on Mark. Enmeshment inevitably generates resentment.

Now that I was able to look at myself with curiosity rather than judgment, I could see how the parts of my unworked trauma had mutated into aggression toward Mark. I had been more focused on what I perceived I wasn't *getting* from my marriage than looking at what I wasn't *giving* to our relationship. Looking at the ways that I had been causing him harm was a crucial shift in my orientation. Through this, I could recognize that Mark kicking me out of the house created this pivotal turning point. How would we have interrupted our habitual dance forged over two decades any other way? I hadn't had any incentive to change my behavior before I was faced with this crisis.

Mark, of course, had his own responsibility in our dynamic. His anger could also come out sideways. He was often forgetful when we made an agreement or unconsciously generated situations to get back at me. But by initiating a therapeutic separation, he was taking the necessary steps to clear up these indirect ways he had been expressing his anger and resentment. Setting this boundary helped him clean up his lane. He was willing to be uncomfortable enough to disrupt the status quo with no guarantees about the results. With this action, he gave us both a chance to grow regardless of the outcome. This was his commitment to our marriage.

It is ironic that sometimes saying "no" is the most relational stance. We don't often associate compassion with boundary setting, but a mature love challenges one's beloved to grow, it holds accountability, it is capable of saying "stop." I could now appreciate the abiding care behind Mark's actions. The forced time apart was the best catalyst for my growth that my husband had ever offered me.

I admire him for the courage that I know it took to disrupt our established dynamic. I didn't know how to fully love, and it took this action to help me look more deeply into what was getting in the way. During one of my therapy sessions, Gary asserted, "We all are innately capable of loving. The important work is studying how we hate. Through this awareness our compassion can flow more freely."

With the enormous help of our therapy group members and Gary, Mark and I recalibrated our relationship. After four months of separation, I moved back in and we forged a new path, one holding, not erasing, the awareness of our history and propensities. We are bound to repeat the past if we forget what it has taught us. It would only be through my maintaining a wakefulness of my knee-jerk tendencies and my own distorted narratives that I would now have a chance at slowing down my reactivity and making other choices in those moments.

Simultaneously, Mark was dedicated to doing his version of this work of breaking his old patterns of conditioning. We both were committed not just to our marriage but to the ongoing work of deepening our awareness of the forces that had come to shape us and therefore enhance our capacity to see ourselves and each other more clearly.

At the same time that my consciousness was going through a profound reconciliation with the past and within my marriage, the culture at large was encountering a similar upheaval. Up to this point, my work on the abuse from my childhood, as it intersected with my life in the present, had been mostly a personal journey. I couldn't have imagined or predicted how the rise of the #MeToo movement in 2017 would serve to uncover the widespread extent of sexual abuse in our culture and forever expand our dialogue about it.

CHAPTER 35

TRANSPORTED
TO VIRGINIA

It was while the #MeToo movement, originally conceived by Tarana Burke, was gaining momentum and continuing to reveal many atrocious abuses of power, that I casually picked up my phone to scroll through the morning news that next spring in Seattle. Mark had left for work, and I was making breakfast before my first client appointment. Suddenly the headline of a *New York Times* article splayed me open like the eggs I had just cracked into the frying pan. *Behind an Equestrian Legend, A Legacy of Abuse*, it read. In an instant these capitalized words catapulted me once again from my tree-lined urban street back three thousand miles to the horse-infused countryside of my childhood. In a momentary whoosh, this headline leapt out of my phone screen and tightened itself around my jugular, leaving me shaking for breath.

The article conveyed an eerily similar version of my own story. This predatory abuser was a renowned California horse trainer who, over decades, likewise bulldozed through many young girls' lives. Same era, same unanswerable arrogance, same lack of accountability. Other arenas had been coughing up their own secrets. Now it had just blown the lid off old festering abuses in the equestrian world too.

I had already begun to write my story in memoir form, but feeling a strong kinship with those in this article, I was inspired to offer what I could from my own history with a more immediate response. I sat down that day, and a letter of solidarity tumbled out onto the pages. It was intended to validate those women who had bravely come forward to name their abusive trainer. I wanted them to know that I was grateful for their voices, their courage. I wanted to join my name to theirs as we marched out of the silence together.

I wrote my own parallel memory of that time when I, too, had found myself cornered in a horse stall, my back against the wall, fending off unwelcome kisses with nowhere to go. I described how my love of horses was likewise used as weapon leveraged by a perpetrator. The words wove quickly into sentences. It was cathartic.

Now what? I wanted to put it out in the world but wasn't sure how to go about that.

"Try going back to the source," suggested Gary.

"Is there a place to publish it in your hometown?" he asked. I hadn't been back to Virginia since ending contact with Clarentine, but read that he had died in the interim. I didn't know if the local newspaper I knew in my childhood was still even serving that community, but it seemed like a good place to start.

While initially I was able to reach a friendly editor, after I sent her a copy of what I had written, her response to me cooled. With a formality that she didn't originally have, she informed me that she would have to talk with her managing editor and get back to me. Later that day, she concluded that it would be too difficult for the newspaper to print this piece. The stated reason was that this article was a liability risk and would be too burdensome for their fact-checking staff to take on. After all, they didn't have a large team like the *NYT* that would be needed for this task.

"Needed for what?" I inquired, not yet understanding. She skirted around the issue until finally stating directly that this small newspaper didn't have the resources to fight any possible defamation lawsuits that they worried my piece might inflame.

I took a stab at an argument. "But he's already dead. Besides, don't I have a right to write about my own experience? Can't the truth be published?"

I thought, if there are no publishers willing to take risks in support of their authors' victim experiences, how can these stories ever be told? Doesn't this just perpetuate the problem further? The lack of access to media exposure amounts to just more of the same—protecting the predator, colluding in the silencing, maintaining the existing power base. I respectfully tried to air these points, knowing that any further debate would be moot. The decision had been made. She apologized. I understood. I was muzzled by a similar bargain for the majority of my life, but I wasn't going to be stopped by that now. I went looking for allies elsewhere.

Next, I turned to *The Chronicle of the Horse*. It was and still is one of the most recognized magazines serving a diverse equestrian readership in the country. Growing up, this publication was printed in black and white and was considerably thinner in volume, but even then it offered coverage of horse news, show results, and related articles involving all forms of equestrian pursuits. As children, my friend Kit and I had pored over the grainy photos of horse and rider jumping pairs and pictures of those collecting their winning ribbons in the ring during pre-show sleepovers at her house. She had a subscription, and we followed the rising horseback riding stars in the *COTH* like avid fans tracked movie celebrities in *People* magazine.

When I reached out, a person at the magazine actually answered the phone and greeted me warmly when I told her the purpose of my call. She immediately put me in touch with their head editor with assurances that they were interested in my story. In the course of our conversation, I discovered that not only did this national equestrian magazine dedicate a whole recent issue to #MeToo, as it sadly but predictably impacted the world of horses, but it also had continually been offering a platform for open discussion and disagreement about the handling of reported abuses. In some instances, this meant absorbing difficult pushback from the unpopular calling out of abuses by horse trainers who had previously held iconic positions in the equestrian world.

Although they said they would also have to run it by their team of lawyers before publishing, they assured me that they supported me and would publish as much of it as they could. Their legal advisors counseled the magazine to not publish any major identifying facts, such as his name or the specific location of the stables. However, the editors pushed to let me name the state and keep many of the descriptive details about him that existed in my original version.

When they told me about these relatively minor editorial restrictions, I still took a moment to consider if this was enough. They were generous indeed, but was I compromising in my effort to get the full facts published? Was I settling in ways that I shouldn't? But I quickly decided that this was an important start to sharing my story. And I was working on writing a memoir anyway. Besides, I knew that anyone who had met Clarentine and read my piece would know who I was talking about from the unmistakable descriptors I was able to retain. It turned out that I was right, but it still surprised me when I started hearing from others from my riding past.

CHAPTER 36

RECONNECTING WITH "ONE OF THE GIRLS"

Julie, like me, had always loved horses. We grew up in the same neighborhood and rode at the barn. We weren't close back then. She wasn't one of his open jumper riders, so our circles, even at our small barn, were somewhat different. Also, there were too many other forces at work separating all of us from one another, but we shared a deep affection for horses and a knotted history with Clarentine, so hearing from her felt like a sacred offering.

She told me that when she read my piece in *The Chronicle of the Horse*, she wanted to contact me and yet understandably hesitated. It took her a good part of a week and several days off work before she was able to bravely muster up the courage to track me down and send a follow-up email. Not only had it been forty-plus years, but talking about life at the stables would be going against our old prime directive. I'd felt this invisible constraint when I wrote the piece, and she was feeling it now when contacting me.

"It was such a weird coincidence." She began by recounting the story of how she came to hear about my article. Working as a nurse in a local hospital, she was helping a patient who was recovering from day surgery. When she went to retrieve this older woman's clothes for her discharge, the woman apologized. "Sorry they smell like manure. I wanted to get in a morning ride, so I came straight from the horse barn."

"I used to ride, too, so not a problem," Julie said, assuring her that she was familiar with this nostalgic aroma. To riders, horse shit quickly takes on a positive olfactory association.

"Well, since you once rode around here, maybe you can answer the question that my friends and I have been trying to figure out. There was this #MeToo story about an abusive trainer in the latest *COTH*, and we can't figure out who it was. Sounds like he owned a horse barn somewhere here in Virginia." This woman went on to share some of the descriptive details that were included in my story: "A gold tooth . . . and always wore a knife at his side." With this, Julie reflexively gasped.

"I know exactly who that was!" she managed to blurt out. "He used to call that knife his wife."

Julie was not surprised when her patient asked if she could write down Clarentine's name. She and I both knew that no one could remember it when they first heard it. After her shift, she looked up my published piece, found my web page, and gathered the means to contact me directly. Then she balked. Contending with the past would be a Herculean act of courage. Choosing to dredge up uncomfortable, painful feelings goes against the grain for us all. But she pushed through this in herself and reached out. I am so grateful she did. We arranged a time to talk via a phone call.

Without choosing it, back then we all implicitly agreed to not speak aloud about the various forms of sexual abuse happening during this formative time in our lives. Collectively, we were complicit in the suppression and denial. This conditioned code of silence isolated us. It is one more way that trauma carries a lasting impact. I imagine that other riders, like me, remembered the horses, the freedom we felt atop of our favorites, but tried to bury, deny, or repackage the rest. Out of misplaced loyalty, it became easier for me to remember Clarentine for this access to the horses that he gave and try to forget or minimize what he took, the price he demanded and exacted.

Hearing her voice on the other end, I knew that we were going to be bridging this divide. This would be the first time either of us would be speaking directly to someone who shared this past.

There was an initial awkwardness. Without stating it, we both needed to work our way into talking about him and the abuse. We started with our mothers. Julie, like me, had confronted her mother many years back. Her experience didn't go any better than my own.

When she opened up to her mom about Clarentine's abuse, rather than being able to hear the terror that her daughter lived through, her mother instead responded, "Well, I'm sure you didn't mean to, but you must have somehow led him on." She followed this by insistently defending that she had no idea what was happening at the barn.

During this same conversation, Julie pressed her by taking a different tack and asked her if she had ever sensed anything scary about Clarentine. It was then that her mother admitted that she recalled a time when together the two of them had to ride in the van with him in order to transport Julie's horse somewhere. Her mother confessed, "I didn't feel at all comfortable with him because he was naked from the waist up." Julie countered with incredulity, "So you made me sit next to him?!"

Then her mother gave a telling response. "Well, I figured you were more used to him."

Julie and I continued to share our stories with accelerated scattershot. We talked about how we had each dealt with life since. She had become a nurse, I, a therapist. We had both done work on our past trauma in therapy. We agreed that trauma is not something that one gets over. It is something that one works with—layer by layer. We both had had to cast off the misplaced burden of responsibility for what had happened to us. We both had to rewrite our false narratives.

We knew that there were many of us riders who hadn't been able to engage in this difficult work. Through the years, Julie had tried to bring it up with some of those who were still in the area but was met with varying degrees of resistance—and their persistent loyalty to Clarentine.

"The past is the past."

"It wasn't so bad."

"I just wanted to let him finish out his life in peace."

"He was just an old man by the end."

These were some of the party line refrains she heard. One rider even reached out to Julie at some point to persuade her to go see him because his days were numbered. "Just go visit him. He shouldn't have to be alone."

I had held onto very similar loyalties for a long time. It is so threatening at the deepest cellular layer to try to dislodge an already precarious narrative. It requires letting go of the old protective storylines and, like glass vases in an earthquake, allowing them to shatter on the ground in broken, sharp bits.

It's much more appealing to stay caught up in the falsified story rather than address the reality of the abuse full-on.

"My therapist called it a cult," Julie then shared.

"Oh my God!" I responded. "Mine did too!" And so our healing conversation deepened. I was speaking to someone who knew what had happened, had a similar experience with Clarentine . . . who remembered what it was like. We were fellow cult members, and talking about this even now, in our adult bodies, with lives far removed from the past, still felt forbidden and risky. We were breaking the rules. We were breaking the shackles.

Julie proceeded to tell me about the constant pressure she was forced to endure back then. The bribes, the horse that she longed for, the lack of parental support, the wish that it would all stop, the promise that it would be just that once . . . a nightmare relived as she and her body faded further into oblivion with each subsequent time.

"I went to confront him a few years before he died." She whispered this almost like a confession. "Even though my therapist recommended against it, I felt it was something I needed to do."

I took in a sharp breath. "Whoa, how did that go?"

In search of a reckoning, she decided to seek him out. She didn't even know if he was still living at the stables, but one day she drove to the old location to find out. Sure enough, Clarentine was there. As she tells it, he had aged significantly, and it was clear right away that his mind was going to pasture. He didn't recognize her even after she told him who she was. She bravely forged ahead with her plan to confront him about what he had done to her anyway, what he had taken from her as a young girl, how his abuse had impacted her. Perhaps the truth, she reasoned, would jog his faltering memory.

He said it never happened, that he didn't know what she was going on about. But she observed that he appeared agitated even while denying everything. While he was talking, he hinged from the waist closer in Julie's direction. She leaned back. Then, with what appeared to be a perverse sense of enjoyment, he began to share grisly details about the three men he had killed in his life. She noticed that at the same time he kept swishing one free hand under his chair like he was distractedly searching for something he had lost. Odd, a demented man's quirkiness, she thought at first.

Then, all of a sudden, it hit her like a rasp to the head. He was looking for his gun! The one he always kept nearby, whether in the van, the tack room, or possibly now under the chair where he was currently sitting.

Turning ashen in that instant of comprehension, she jumped up, sprinted to her car, and, with her body quivering from head to toe, peeled out down the driveway.

"Oh my God, how scary! I am so sorry." My own nervous system was vicariously triggered just imagining the scene she was describing.

We both had grown up around this constant threat of danger. It was ever-present, and yet we each grew adept at tamping it down. We were always on the tightrope of what was going to happen next and became accustomed, to the point of wearied numbness, to the loaded guns that were never far away. But our bodies remembered, even as our disconnected selves learned not to pay attention.

This first conversation with Julie, along with our subsequent ones, was a healing balm. Writing about my childhood experience and talking about it in therapy and with friends was one thing and has been fundamental to my journey. However, the gift of being able to speak aloud with someone who shares a similar history took vulnerability and validation to a whole new level. We continued to witness each other's telling of truths, healing decades of imposed silence. Throughout our sharing, I could feel my body habitually clench in old patterns of protection, then, in the next breath, gently loosen amid the confirmation.

The common history we separately lived had pixelated us, but now, by opening it up into the light with each other, we were mosaic-ing ourselves back together again.

CHAPTER 37

RETURNING HOME

Virginia is in my blood, not my born blood, but the critical time of young girlhood blood. It is the place of lost and found for me—where I found my love of horses and my sense of courage and strength, and where I lost my innocence and connection to myself. It had been twenty-four years since I had last stepped foot in Charlottesville. During that visit, I had seen Clarentine for the last time. Soon afterward, I wrote him the letter that severed our relationship and all further contact.

Since that time, I had embarked on my new life in Seattle. I had evolved personally through my own therapy while my professional work as a therapist likewise deepened. I was continuing to learn what it meant to be in a truly mutual partnership with Mark. Our marriage was vastly stronger because of the work we had both been doing, so by the time the #MeToo movement and the *NYT* article reopened my past, I was already in my fifties. My parents had moved away from the area, and there had been no incentive to return to Virginia. Now, going home felt timely. I had another layer to peel back. This would involve returning to the origin of my abuse.

That final time I had seen Clarentine, I was still living in the alternate reality of my own making. How convenient it was back then to think that I had successfully navigated around a predator. There was something for me to rediscover and reclaim now in returning to my hometown on my own terms, under my own initiative, having shed this old story. There was something that I needed to reconcile in order to further integrate the present within the context of the past. Sometimes the next layer of work requires one to go back in order to move forward. I wondered what it would be like to go home after so long. What does this even mean?

My plan included revisiting my childhood home, the neighborhood, the old Ivy Store, and what, if anything, still existed of the stables. I would be returning to the scene of the crimes—both literally and emotionally. I knew from Clarentine's obituary that he had died ten years before. It was his ghost I would be confronting.

With my plans crystallized and my ticket bought, horses began trotting into my dreams again. This used to happen regularly, but over time, dreams involving horses occurred less and less. Now, on the brink of traveling back to Virginia, horses again starred in my night visions. In one, I was leading a horse out of a storage unit, knowing that he shouldn't be kept there and that he didn't belong in an industrial zone. I was looking for a green pasture where this animal could freely graze. So obvious, right? I was emotionally taking horses out of mothballs by returning to Virginia.

Driving the two and a half hours toward my past from D.C.'s Dulles airport, I felt jittery behind the wheel in anticipation of retracing the footsteps of my history. I reminded myself that I was the one in the driver's seat. Unlike before, I now had agency over this next chapter.

I braced myself for it all to look different, fearing that the rural landscape would have changed beyond recognition, but the creeping concrete progress that I had dreaded hadn't swallowed up the countryside at all. The farmland still had room to stretch out its green legs along generous parcels of acreage demarcated by those same wooden fences. Just like before, the natural beauty of this area bathed my eyes in all directions, filling me with nostalgia.

The trees represented the biggest change. These silent witnesses had grown much more towering with the years. These majestic oaks and sycamores canopied toward each other with reaching limbs in peaceful gestures across the now more shaded roads that wove below. I was surprised by how comforted I felt seeing this familiar flora and fauna paint this landscape. Even the ominous vultures owning the sky in circling arcs were a welcomed sight. But especially seeing the grazing horses in the fields as I drove by rekindled a deep sense of affection I had almost forgotten.

Ironically, while revisiting this countryside to find my Airbnb, I lost GPS and phone coverage just as I passed the old Ivy Store. Not knowing how to locate where I would be staying, I'd now have to ask for directions the old-fashioned way. As I turned the rental car around to park in front of the store, it wasn't lost on me that I would be walking into the scene of that old murder. The stars were certainly aligning to help me revisit the past. Ready or not.

As I walked again across the threshold, I was surprised to find that it was basically the same small country store. So little had changed. At the checkout counter in a small wicker basket were John's (or were they Pete's?) homegrown labeled peaches casually huddled together. I grabbed a few to purchase while I asked for directions.

The clerk had a general idea. Walking me outside, he gestured for me to take a right immediately after the railroad trestle in the distance. He instructed that I follow it for a time then take a left at the second curve . . . and so on. Locations are found by natural landmarks and the number of bends in the road. This had to suffice out here, as nothing was laid out or labeled by a city grid with perpendicular streets and avenues. I thanked him, paid for my fresh fruit, and headed up the road "a piece."

Over the next week, I began to retrace other familiar haunts of my past. Christina, my old college roommate, who was living on the East Coast, offered to accompany me on this pilgrimage. It was so helpful to have the presence and perspective of a dear friend along the way. That was the big difference in general for me between then and now. I no longer needed to go it alone.

Entering the sprawling subdivision where I grew up, we drove through the neighborhood, first to my childhood home. The outside of the house itself hadn't been altered. The brickwork didn't look any worse for wear. The giant stand-alone bell that would toll for me to return from the barn at the end of the day still occupied space off to one side of the house. Except for the magnified height of the trees in the yard, it looked as though time had pushed pause.

From the top of this familiar knoll, I gazed down the hill. My eye traced across the fields I had traversed so many countless times en route to the stables. The large old barn structure was still visible, but it was hard to tell from this angle how much of the rest of the buildings remained intact. I was about to find out.

Driving up that driveway was like being pelted by a hailstorm from the past. Dense nuggets of memory rained down on me from all directions. When we reached the top of the drive, what we used to call the lower barn came into view. As if held in suspended animation, it also surprisingly appeared the same. The old tack room had obviously been adopted as someone's main living space, but the original footprint had been kept intact. The fields were still fenced as they once were. The upper barn was falling down, but not more than it ever was. Although the fencing of the riding ring had been removed, the space that it used to occupy remained visibly still compressed by years of hoof beats. It was surreal to find so much unchanged.

However, what was starkly missing in this rendition were the horses. They were the life of the stables and the pulse of my connection. In their absence, it was like viewing a lifeless shell trapped in amber long after the last breath had been drawn. I realized that this place held no power over me anymore.

CHAPTER 38

REUNITING
WITH HORSES

The next day I looked up another old friend who had also grown up riding horses in the area. We met at a café a short distance from the stables. While nibbling our luncheon salads, we easily bridged the gap of decades afforded by old familiarity.

Louise, like many people living in the country at that time, had kept horses in her backyard on a casual basis. Horses, in this part of the world, were often considered beloved family pets alongside outdoor dogs, cats, chickens, and goats. She always rode for herself, never for Clarentine, but like everyone back then, she certainly knew him. Unlike me, she kept her distance. She shared with me that she had always felt terrified of him. She told me she never would have considered riding for him. She found him too scary and intimidating. Whenever she happened to find herself crossing paths with him at the show-grounds, she would cut a wide swath between him and her.

I sighed. Being in his presence required me to disconnect from myself. Here was another bit of evidence exposing the necessary self-annihilation of my own authentic response to the danger I employed in order to spend time at the barn with these animals I loved.

I had rarely spoken about Clarentine's abuse and never to Louise, but now, in person, I shared the personal impact of my experience at the barn. I told her of the *New York Times* article that hit particularly close to home and that had prompted me to write a response for *COTH*. I revealed that it was time for me to come back and untangle more of my past.

As our conversation continued to deepen, I was surprised to learn that she had just retired from her longtime job of running the riding program at a small women's college in order to start her own equine therapy business!

I had always felt a surge of warmth whenever I heard about horses being invited to aid in the healing of those suffering from trauma. I completely understood how this burgeoning field would be beneficial to all traumatized groups: military veterans, struggling youth, prisoners, those suffering with addictions and all forms of abuse. We both knew of the numerous studies that have been conducted in the decades since I left the world of horses explaining why horses are such natural co-therapists.

Louise went on to describe the opening exercise she uses for her intensive weekends. She asks the participants to sit quietly in the middle of the corral while the horses roam freely around them. For those not already familiar and comfortable in the presence of horses, this in itself can elicit a direct confrontation with one's fear.

Each participant is then challenged to wait patiently and allow a horse, in their own time, to choose them. This struck me as such a powerful practice requiring one to literally sit with one's anxiety and surrender to the vulnerability of waiting to be chosen. Through this icebreaker, Louise related how the seeds of mutual trust and connection between human and horse are magically sown.

When I asked her how she came by these special horses, she told me that this was ad hoc. She had some horses that had never experienced abuse at the hands of humans. Their trust levels were innately high, so their responses were unhindered. In contrast, she came to host other horses that had been severely beaten. Traumatic experiences, just like with people, had cut them off from their authentic emotions. These horses were given a safe environment where, over time, trust could be rebuilt. It was apparent that she was running a rehab farm—for humans as well as horses.

Louise's approach reflected her exquisite respect for these animals. She no longer bought, sold, or traded up. Her philosophy was to partner with them as co-facilitators. Honoring that they brought their own wisdom to bear on any situation, they were never used as instruments in the process. Rather she allowed space for them to choose if and how they wanted to participate.

Horses had always provided an emotional connection for me in my childhood, even when Clarentine was sabotaging it. They gave me a lifeline, but I had to go through him in order to be with them. Back then, I couldn't afford to lose the friendships that these horses offered. And yet being in proximity to the barn meant that I had to cauterize the connection to myself. This was my childhood bind. When I was finally able to dissect myself from Clarentine, I had to walk away from it all. Horses were the collateral damage.

Hearing Louise speak about this reignited the seed of my own longing to reconnect with my original love for these incredible creatures.

CHAPTER 39

THE JOURNEY
CONTINUES

Some months after I had returned to Seattle, I had another riveting horse dream. The details were ephemeral, but I awoke filled with the sensation of horses all around me. I don't know how else to describe it. It kindled in me a strong longing to take action to mend this old split I had with horses. I contacted Louise the very next morning, and she generously encouraged me to come experience her horses and her farm in Virginia. My last journey back was to confront the ghost of Clarentine. I hoped that this trip would help me repair my equine relationships.

I believe that there are two personal reckonings of the highest magnitude in the quest to know ourselves. Recognizing how we have been impacted by our traumas, including the stories we tell ourselves as a result, and reconciling the ways that we have caused harm to others. For me, horses were associated with both. In their presence, I had been both victimized and violent. This wasn't a proportionate equation, but I knew I needed to come to terms with both sets of internalized experiences.

CAROL ODELL

I had been taking responsibility for how this showed up in my interactions with Mark and others. Now this journey would focus on making amends for the hurt I had caused horses in the past. I hoped that being around horses again would also reconnect me to the deep love and appreciation for them that had been compromised. With this intention, I booked my flight and headed back to the Charlottesville area for a second time in fairly quick succession.

This is how I now found myself standing on the edge of an expansive paddock, looking at eight swishy-tailed horses grazing on hay a midfield distance away. Louise and her husband, Jace, owned Bent Post Farm, a gorgeous parcel of land that was cradled in the foothills of the Blue Ridge Mountains, and I was about to immerse myself in a few days of equine therapy here in this resonant setting.

Standing just inside the entrance to this field, Louise began by inviting me to pay attention to each horse's subtle response to my presence. Celie was the first to take notice of me. Louise told me that she was the leader of this group and as such she kept watch for the entire herd. To my eyes, she raised her head and gave me only a quick sideways glance, but Louise reminded me that the bulk of horses' vision is peripheral. Celie went back to eating, so she had determined that I wasn't a threat.

While quietly observing for subtle shifts in the other horses' behaviors, we were waiting to see if any chose to approach me on their terms. My stomach tightened. Would any horse come to greet me? What if none did? Fear of rejection is such a core human dread. It boiled down to *Am I worthy?* I could feel the question viscerally pulsing through me in this moment, making it hard to stand still and patiently wait.

Bill, the handsome chestnut, made the first move when he began a slow walking-while-eating meandering path in my direction. Horses don't operate on human time, so he was in no particular hurry. He finally sauntered right up to me and stole my heart that first day with his playful energy. Having only known kindness, he easily trusted humans. Like a four-hooved Peter Pan, he was perpetually young at heart, provided comic relief, tested the boundaries, and was mischievous and curious about everything. And he expected to get away with his antics. He was hard to resist. Most importantly in that moment, though, he had chosen me. I had been accepted into the herd.

The next morning, Louise directed Bill and me into the ring to do some natural work on the flat. I was told that today's session would focus on inhabiting right leadership, but I wasn't sure what was in store for me. "Horses want a leader," Louise began. "As herd animals, they are innately oriented to be cooperative and work in harmony. But becoming a leader is an earned position."

What is right leadership? How do we learn to inhabit our power? Especially when we have been impacted by the misuse of power?

What I had learned about authority from Clarentine only involved domination and intimidation. Power often felt like a dirty word for me. I associated it with forced obedience, a demand to control at all costs, an obliteration of sovereign choice. Brené Brown brilliantly clarifies this difference as "power with" in contrast to "power over."

My past negative experiences of power sometimes made it dicey for me to know how to step into the right leadership with others. Not dominating but also not shrinking from this role was not always an easy middle path for me. I had painfully become aware of how I assumed a superior stance in my marriage with Mark. Now I was going to try to enact a new form of leadership with a horse as my mentor.

First, Louise positioned me at Bill's shoulder. I was told this was the "drive line" and the place from where I would be leading. In my old way of leading a horse, I would have stood in front of him and given a tug on the lead line. She was suggesting something completely foreign. Louise taught me that a horse's acceptance of another's leadership is exhibited through their hooves, not the head. Getting a horse to move its legs was the confirmation we were looking for.

Then, Louise posed the assignment, "So now I want you and Bill to walk around the ring, side by side, using only your intent."

"What do you mean?"

"Energetically set an intention so he knows what you are asking."

"How do I do that?"

Louise instructed me to start by affirming the goal, which was for us to walk forward at the same time. Louise directed me to focus my energy on a point on the horizon where I wanted to go and keep my eyes looking there. Then all I needed was to take the first step with a committed faith that Bill would also move with me.

I was suddenly aware of my concern that he might not follow me. That worry made my first step a hesitant one. I also insecurely looked down at his hoof to see if he was planning to come along. Having received my ambivalent message loud and clear, he didn't budge. This perfectly reflected my reluctant leadership in that moment! Wanting to make up for at times being too harsh in the past, now I had swung too much in the other direction. I was too passive, not communicating clearly what I wanted. By not being assertive enough, he didn't know how to respond.

I had known only "power over" growing up at the barn. I confounded right authority with the dictatorship I had been impacted by. I wanted to be granted leadership without having to earn it. The result was my shying away from my own authority, which only confused my horse, who was ready to see me as a benevolent leader if only I could get my act together. Learning to invite "power with" would be a new skill in this arena.

It was a great exercise to have to find another way within myself—not the old habitual way, but not in reaction to it either. It required trusting the relationship rather than trying to control it or shirk away from it. Hmm, it sounded like a familiar problem that I sometimes experienced elsewhere. With a commitment of faith, I needed to step boldly forward and expect that my horse would step along with me. In my next attempt, he followed my lead.

Everything in that ring revealed other ways that my leadership skills needed work. I had trouble staying at his shoulder and instead kept gravitating toward walking ahead rather than beside him. I found it hard to keep my right hand relaxed, and it was challenging to keep my eyes in line with where I wanted to go rather than look at him. Louise gently brought these things to my attention.

It was also hard to read when Bill was testing me. When he walked too close to me or nudged me with his head, I wanted to interpret this behavior as him being goofy or having fun. At first, it made me laugh. I even felt flattered by it, but because I didn't define my boundary clearly, he continued to test the limits. Then I didn't like it so much. Without noticing it, I started shrinking my own bubble to accommodate his body moving into our shared space. Bill was looking for a clear leader—otherwise, he wanted to try out the role for himself. If I wasn't going to boldly lead, then he wanted to give it a go.

Louise encouraged me to set firm boundaries with his behavior. The boundary in this case was literally to define a straight plane between us by shimmying my flat hands vertically up and down as if vigorously polishing a door in open space. In this way, I was firmly distinguishing my turf without encroaching on his.

A word about boundary setting. Many abuse survivors have difficulty with boundaries because of the violations suffered. Even those who haven't experienced abuse can also have trouble setting good boundaries. Women in general are acculturated to have relaxed boundaries or none at all. It is a commitment to ourselves to set our own parameters. We all get to decide where our field of space—physically and emotionally—begins and ends. I was now practicing that with my four-hooved, one-ton partner.

Leadership also includes being playful. We ended this session in the ring with a barrel-pushing exercise. By that point,

Bill and I had grown in our horse–woman communication. I was able to convey to Bill that I wanted him to roll a barrel with his nose toward me as I moved backward. It was fun for both of us having this object slowly tumbling between us.

While that day focused on embodying new leadership skills, Louise foreshadowed that the next day would deepen my experience in a different direction.

CHAPTER 40

GRACE

Meditating among free-roaming horses is a unique spiritual practice. When I heard this was how the day would begin, I was excited about the novelty but also felt twinges of nervousness. It would require me to completely surrender. Louise said the focus was to reach out from my heart in connection with theirs and be open to whatever they wanted to offer me. Because her approach is to never use her therapy animals as a means to an end, she never knew what was going to unfold. She trusted that, unlike us humans, horses naturally reside in the present moment and, because of this, they have an innate ability to respond to the energy in the here and now. Powerful wisdom and modeling for us humans who tend to spend the bulk of our time in the past or in the future.

With four large animals meandering around me and Louise overseeing the meditation, I took a seat on the mounting block in the middle of the large enclosure and closed my eyes. I am reminded that we give room to the most miraculous moments whenever we can let go and enter into uncertainty with open palms and open hearts.

I must have dropped into a very deep state of quiet because when Louise let me know that Bill was moving toward me, it felt like I was emerging from a long, peaceful trance. This large chestnut horse walked up to where I sat and nuzzled a smile out of me. He was clearly the jester in my Shakespearean drama.

Noting how the other horses had positioned their bodies, I realized they were giving me the signal of their interest and invitation as well. Louise guided me to walk slowly toward them one at a time and speak to each of them as I was moved to do. Louise observed and translated their body language for me from a distance as I moved to interact with them. All four of these hooved healers offered me precious gifts, but it was Grace who broke open my heart.

Grace was a chunky pinto horse who harbored her own story of abuse at the hands of a violent human. She had been regularly beaten in private, and when her violent owner couldn't sell her at an auction, he whipped her in public. A woman who witnessed this in horror bought Grace on the spot and trailered her to Louise, knowing she would provide a good home for this mare. This dear horse was so stricken with fear of humans when she first arrived that she would shake uncontrollably and nervously pee whenever someone walked toward her. Louise had chosen Grace as one of the horses for me this morning because of our intersecting traumas.

Louise said that I could say what I needed to say, like a horse confessional, and knowing Grace's history, I felt compelled to make amends to her. I had been trained to believe that domination was the way to break a horse and that overpowering any behavior that seemed like resistance was "training." Looking back, it always ran against the grain of my soul, but I had learned to silence that voice by shuttering my heart. On the brink of speaking to this horse, the moral injury of it grabbed me by the throat. Through this humility, I approached her. She turned and, in welcoming response, took two decisive steps toward me. Even this bit of acknowledgment felt like an expression of forgiveness. We stood peacefully facing each other, horse to woman, in quiet communion. At one point, Grace exhaled loudly as if to remind me to keep breathing through this. She was right. Now noticing my shallow breathing, I paused for a deep inhalation and tuned back into my body and the heft of what I felt moved to confess.

Standing beside her, I spoke about how deeply sorry I was for the ways I had inflicted hurt onto horses in the past, for the even more frequent ways that I had been silently complicit with Clarentine's violence. And for the long general list of humanity's abuses against horses—poling, drugging, using harsh bits, pulling manes, racing on undeveloped legs, spurs, chained twitches, gelding without anesthesia, separating mares and foals too early . . .

I also told her I was so sorry for the cruel ways she personally had been treated at the hands of people, for all the pain and betrayal and fear she had endured. All the while her ears were pointing forward, patiently listening while I shared my remorse and regret. She had known humans to be the source of her suffering, and yet here she stood, holding space for this human's pain, my pain. This gift of her attention, which I later learned from Louise was rare, suddenly split me open.

Placing my hands on her welcoming back, her solid, steady body met my backlog of grief. I sobbed against her warm fur.

Tears cascaded down my cheeks for all the hurt I had caused others, for the ways that I had also been hurt, for the resulting disconnect within myself. I shed tears for the other girls at the stable, for what they had had to endure, and the similar sufferings sustained throughout the world. I cried for the rending loss of horses in my life—and now for the unconditional generosity this horse was offering me in this poignant moment.

Through wet eyes, I marveled over the miracle that happens when souls touch.

From early on we all operate from a deep distortion of ourselves. When we believe that the tightly folded bundle we call self is who we actually are, it becomes our foundational pain. This is the false narrative telling us that we somehow aren't enough, that we don't belong, that we aren't worthy. In an attempt to avoid this pain, we hide from ourselves. With courage and intention we can allow this protective—although limiting—shell to dissolve, allowing us to better connect with others through our essential self. One client came up with this mantra as a reminder of this irrefutable fact: "I am worthy because I breathe."

Accepting all of who we are, especially our jaggedness and imperfections, is the very definition of self-forgiveness. When we begin to recognize that we all embody the aggregate suffering of humanity AND the exquisite splendor of our collective essence, then we are integrating the full truth of who we are.

Honoring rather than hating the cracks and crevices that make us human in turn helps us forgive and empathize with others. When we enter into a process of unfolding these accumulated wads of old hurts and fears and limiting narratives, the relief is palpable. Then we can courageously start to unfurl and wave in the wind. This is how we become prayer flags for the world.

These were the tears baptizing me, with Grace as my witness.

"If that wasn't church, I don't know what is," Louise reflected afterward as we thanked and ushered the horses back into their larger paddock.

I left Bent Post Farm the following day feeling alive and expansive. The renewed connection I felt with horses was deeply healing. I was filled with gratitude for this experience, for my community, for the sage, compassionate Grace, for the chance to continue to grow along my journey.

Upon returning to my Seattle home, I laid the last of the broken pieces of porcelain into a large mosaic wall hanging that I had been working on for years. The once disparate collection of shards now completed a whole picture. It depicts a white horse transformed into a Pegasus. Every time I gaze upon it, I see myself astride this sky-soaring creature and imagine that we are together, flying boldly with spread wings into the beautiful unknown.

ACKNOWLEDGMENTS

As a person who once thought I had to go it alone, the importance of community has been a sacred part of my evolution. I won't be able to name everyone here, but please know how deeply appreciative I am of the many ways that all my friends, family, and communities nurture me in mind, body, and spirit with love and laughter. I am so very grateful to you all.

Writing is its own personal quest but one not to be undertaken without a full spectrum of support. Huge thanks go out to Brooke Warner and her incredible team of women including Stephanie, Julie, Krissa, Addison . . . and to my sister authors of She Writes Press for helping me birth this memoir into the world. Heartfelt thanks also to my developmental editor and friend, Gail Hudson, and to Ann Hedreen, my memoir writing teacher/friend. And to all my dear beta reading peeps: Mark, Laurie, Julie, Alison, Bradley, Patty, Jacqui, Anne, Jude, Susan. I appreciate all your insights and reflections. Hearty shout-outs to my publicist, Angelle, at Books Forward. Also to Martha and Alice for their savvy tech support, coaching and friendship.

And to all my fellow Gary-ites, profound thanks for the collective awareness that we laboriously cultivated and offered to each other in our therapy groups those many years. By extension, a special acknowledgment to my courageous clients who continually honor me with their trust and vulnerability. I am humbled and privileged to be walking these many journeys with you.

I also appreciate the communities I am a part of that offer me a welcome balance along the way. Here's to my squash sisters and brothers, as well as my pickleball cohorts, for providing active antidotes to the many hours of sitting in front of a computer screen. With appreciation to my bridge gals, my conscious raising WWWT group, and the fine orators at Wallingford Toastmasters. Special hugs to Claire Barnett and all the Seattle Mosaic Arts studio members for providing a creative atmosphere that augments the written word with tesserae and friendship.

Here's to all the horses that I have known and loved and to all the "girls at the stables" and the beautiful, fierce women you have become. To Louise, deep gratitude for your friendship and the equine-assisted work that you offer in the world. May those in need find you and the Grazia Foundation.

And, of course, my warm affection for my inner circle of dear friends and family. I am so blessed by my extraordinary BFFs and honored to be a sister, a Dragonfly member, a godmother of two remarkable women, and a multiple times over aunt and now great auntie. And thanks, Will, I always knew you were near. I love you all dearly.

Special appreciation to my beloved, my amazing husband, Mark. You are my light, my mirror, my life. I am so grateful to be walking this four-decade journey with you hand in hand. I look forward to all that lies ahead. And much love to you, Connor. I am so humbled to be your mom witnessing you carve your own path through this complicated world.

And lastly, for everyone who may pick up this book along the way, may it remind you that we are all worthy and we are all connected.

ABOUT THE AUTHOR

Mark Smith

Carol Odell, LICSW, grew up riding horses on the show jumping circuit in Virginia.

She has been a practicing psychotherapist facilitating groups and working with couples and individuals since 1984. Married for thirty-eight years and the mother of a grown son, her other passions include: squash, pickleball, partner dancing, mosaics, writing, hiking, traveling, and being in community with friends and family. She and her husband currently split their time between Seattle and Cle Elum, Washington.

Looking for your next great read?

We can help!

Visit www.shewritespress.com/next-read
or scan the QR code below for a list
of our recommended titles.

She Writes Press is an award-winning
independent publishing company founded to
serve women writers everywhere.